T0248183

Praise for *Awaken Your Potential*...

Awaken Your Potential sounds a clarion call to action for anyone tired of settling for less than their best. My friend Chad Reyes knows firsthand how fulfilling your unique purpose requires practicing habits that transform good intentions into great accomplishments. Drawing on his own experience and wisdom gleaned from top-tier leaders and personal mentors, Chad offers fresh perspective on timeless principles guaranteed to ignite, inspire, and illuminate your view of leadership.

—Chris Hodges, Senior Pastor, Church of the Highlands, and Author of *Out of the Cave* and *Pray First*

This book is a must-read for those who desire to learn timeless principles that align with ancient treasure troves of wisdom that have shaped Western civilization. I highly recommend it!

—Dr. Joseph Mattera, Author and Leadership Consultant, Mattera Global

Awaken Your Potential is a captivating journey into the world of effective leadership and personal growth. Chad's storytelling, enriched with his own experiences, transforms this book into a compelling page-turner. It's more than theory; it's a treasure trove of practical concepts, a true playbook for anyone eager to correct their path to success. The actionable insights provided in this book are invaluable for those aspiring to lead and live a more fulfilled life.

—Farid Abdelkader, CEH, CDPSE, CISA, CISSP, CRISC, CSX, CISM, Executive Officer of the ISACA Metropolitan New York Chapter, and Global Head of Technology Audit at New York Life Insurance Company

Chad's playbook for personal development goes beyond traditional success stories, offering principles that serve as foundational building blocks for generating momentum. *Awaken Your Potential* is essential reading for those committed to reaching the next level, whether personally or in the workplace.

—Nigel James, Renowned Industry Veteran and Visionary Leader in Global Financial Services

Chad's book eloquently meshes the thread between theoretical wisdom and actionable advice. It has universal applicability to make it an invaluable asset to anyone looking to elevate their life both personally and professionally. I will share with administrators across the country!

—Dr. Marion Wilson, NYC Department of Education Superintendent, District 31

It's rare in life that you meet a friend who becomes your role model. Chad is a natural-born leader, and his selflessness and desire to help others is infectious. A must-read for leaders of all levels. Collectively we all make an impact in people's lives.

—Joshua Chananie, CPA, Partner and Service Leader in Top 100 Accounting Firm SAX LLP

Awaken Your Potential and the thoughtful leadership lessons that Chad shares offer a wake-up call for rethinking what leadership means to you and provide a roadmap for transforming your business and the lives around you.

—Charles N. Internicola, Esq., Founder of Internicola Law Firm and Franchise Counsel for Emerging Brands

AWAKEN

YOUR

POTENTIAL

10 WAYS TO
UNLOCK GREATNESS

BY CHAD L. REYES

Forefront
BOOKS

Published by Forefront Books, Nashville, Tennessee.
Distributed by Simon & Schuster.

Unless otherwise indicated, Scripture quotations are from the Holy Bible, New International Version®, NIV®, Copyright © 1973, 1978, 1984, 2011 by Biblica, Inc.™ Used by permission of Zondervan. All rights reserved worldwide.

Library of Congress Control Number: 2023924651
Print ISBN: 978-1-63763-279-6
E-book ISBN: 978-1-63763-280-2

Cover Design by Bruce Gore, Gore Studio, Inc.
Interior Design by Interior Design by PerfecType, Nashville, TN

Printed in the United States of America

This book is dedicated to my amazing wife, best friend, and business and purpose partner, Danielle Reyes. We have been through so much together over the past thirty years, and I am so thankful to God to have you in my life. I am looking forward to seeing how God will continue to use us to impact tens of millions of lives over the next thirty years. As we always say, it's the crazy ones who change the world!

CONTENTS

CONTENTS

FOREWORD

By John C. Maxwell

I've spent most of my life on a journey toward personal and leadership development. Along the way I've had the honor of meeting countless individuals committed to unlocking their full potential. When God first brought Chad and Danielle into my life, I recognized our shared vision: a deep love for people and a genuine desire to add value to their lives. That's why it's no surprise to me that Chad's debut book bears the title *Awaken Your Potential*. What a great title.

Over the years, Chad and Danielle have become beautiful friends of mine. Together, we've traveled the world, witnessed firsthand the transformation of countless lives, and seen the direct impact of our life work. Chad's book is such a natural extension of this mission.

Chad is a talented thought leader passionately dedicated to helping others. I love his personal motto, "Die empty," because it encapsulates the art of living a life brimming with purpose by realizing one's full potential. This aspiration of self-discovery, growth, and resilience is at the heart of *Awaken Your Potential*. I find Chad's writing extremely helpful, as he shares compelling narratives, practical guidance, and profound wisdom. As you read, you'll come to understand that your potential knows no bounds.

Chad's passion for empowering others leaps from every page. He possesses a unique gift for making complex concepts accessible and relatable. That's what really sets his book apart. I'm confident that you will find Chad and his message to be truly impactful, guiding you toward becoming the best version of yourself. Reading his words will be much like having a mentor and guide accompany you on the journey to awaken your potential. Each chapter is filled with actionable steps that can be readily applied to both your personal and professional life, helping you harness your strengths, overcome obstacles, and nurture a growth mindset.

I urge you to approach this resource with an open heart and a willingness to embrace change. Keep in mind that your potential is not a fixed destination; it's an ongoing pursuit throughout your lifetime. We all have the capacity to unleash hidden talents, pursue our dreams, and leave an undeniable mark on the world. In *Awaken Your Potential*, you'll discover how to become the person you were uniquely designed to be.

This book will inspire, challenge, and empower you. It's my genuine pleasure to provide this foreword. I'm thankful for how Chad's friendship has enriched my life, and I'm confident that anyone who reads these pages will experience a similar sense of gratitude.

Chad, your unwavering dedication to helping others reach their fullest potential inspires me. And I am proud to call you my friend.

INTRODUCTION

by Danielle Reyes

Leadership is undoubtedly one of the most complex journeys someone can embark on. While accumulating wealth and power can enhance your status and strength, those things do not equate to leadership. You may inherit a significant amount of money and "things," but leadership is not a legacy that can simply be passed down to you.

In this modern age, there is an urgent need for effective and competent leadership. We are in the midst of a leadership crisis, a serious issue that is prevalent worldwide. The most pressing need globally is not only for financial resources, social programs, or government reforms, but also for leadership that upholds the highest ethical standards, practices self-discipline, and has principled values.

Moreover, this leadership challenge involves awakening the potential within individuals. True leaders not only demonstrate remarkable qualities but also have the ability to inspire and unlock the potential in others. They understand that leadership is not just about their own capabilities but about empowering those around them to realize their fullest potential.

Awakening someone's potential involves recognizing their strengths, encouraging their growth, and providing opportunities for their development. This genuine, authentic leadership, capable of awakening potential, is desperately needed in every aspect of society—government organizations, businesses, educational institutions, civic organizations, youth groups, faith communities, households—and in every area of life.

Unfortunately, as the demand for authentic leadership grows, the task of identifying individuals who embody these traits becomes increasingly challenging. The potential to transform society and instigate positive change depends on our ability to identify and nurture this type of leadership.

In a world full of untapped opportunities, the concept of *potential* is often misunderstood and overlooked. Potential represents the dormant power within us, the inherent ability to evolve, adapt, and overcome our current limitations. It is the source of our yet-to-be-realized talents and capabilities, the dormant qualities that define who we can become.

However, merely having potential is not enough; it must be awakened. *Awakening* refers to the process of recognizing and consciously nurturing this hidden potential within ourselves and others. It involves a journey of self-discovery, growth, and transformation that enables us to unlock our maximum capabilities.

In this book, we will embark on a journey to explore the depths of your potential, discover the secrets to awakening it, and learn how to apply this newfound power to create a life filled with purpose, satisfaction, and influence. Prepare to embark on a transformative journey that not only will change your perception of yourself but also reshape the trajectory of your life.

As you read this book, you will navigate a series of carefully designed chapters, each meticulously crafted to guide you through the critical stages of recognizing, nurturing, and harnessing your inherent potential. Starting with the pivotal distinction between "Good Intentions versus Intentionally Good," moving on to the essential principle of "We Must Value People to Add Value to People," and culminating in the empowering finale of "Fulfill Your Potential and Die Empty," each chapter will provide you with actionable insights and practical exercises specifically designed to awaken your dormant potential and transform it into meaningful, positive results.

The journey will take you through profound lessons about purpose, giving, making commitments, leadership, and more. By the end of your journey, you will not only have a deeper understanding of your own potential but also will have been given the essential tools to activate and utilize it, empowering you to lead a life characterized by growth, accomplishment, and lasting impact.

OUR JOURNEY

In the early days of our journey into entrepreneurship, Chad and I were full of passion and determination. We had a vision to make a positive impact on the world by empowering others to realize their full potential. Despite our enthusiasm and commitment, the path was laden with numerous challenges as we navigated the complexities of starting and growing a business.

In the beginning, we ran a traditional life insurance business. It was a field that promised stability and prosperity, but it was also incredibly competitive and demanding. As new entrants in the market, we struggled to differentiate ourselves from established firms. We had a desire to offer something unique, something that embodied the needs and desires of our clients.

The struggle was real, and we were not working effectively together or even working on the same team. Recognizing the need for guidance from someone with experience and expertise, we decided to invest in a business coach. We needed someone who could help us refine our vision, develop a strategic plan, and equip us with the tools and skills necessary to succeed.

Our coach, a seasoned entrepreneur with a track record of success, quickly became a mentor and confidant. With a gentle yet firm hand, he challenged both of our belief systems, encouraged us to think creatively, and held us accountable for our actions. He helped us understand the importance of listening to our clients, truly understanding their needs and desires, and developing solutions that addressed those needs in a meaningful way.

Empowered by his guidance, Chad and I embarked on an intentional shift to create the business model we had envisioned. We realized that our true passion is in empowering others—not just in selling insurance products but also in focusing on generational planning, helping families create a legacy that would benefit future generations. This shift in focus led to the creation of Wealth & Legacy Group, a generational planning firm with a focus on being Tax Efficient, Legacy Minded, and putting Families First.

Along this journey, our coach helped us develop our leadership skills. He taught us the importance of self-awareness, of understanding our strengths and weaknesses, and of continuously striving for self-improvement. He helped us develop a leadership style that was authentic, empowering, and effective. This journey of self-discovery and growth not only made us better leaders but also better partners, both in business and in life.

The experience was transformative. It helped us refine our vision, develop a strategic plan, and acquire the skills and tools necessary to succeed. It also helped us develop as leaders and as individuals.

Today, we are passionate advocates for the power of coaching and mentorship. Our vision has not wavered; it has evolved into cofounding Lions Pride Leadership and our nonprofit I AM Empowering. Through these efforts, we have dedicated our lives to helping others realize their full potential and make a positive impact on the world.

I am profoundly proud of my husband for his incredible journey and the impact he's making through the work he does. His dedication and discipline in all aspects of his life are truly inspiring. He doesn't just preach about reaching one's potential; he lives it out every day. He embodies the principles he teaches, and I've had the privilege to witness firsthand how his commitment to purpose-driven entrepreneurship, leadership, and personal development has transformed not only his life but also the lives of those around him. Seeing him pour his heart into his initiatives, coach others with genuine care, and consistently strive to be a better version of himself fills me with admiration and love.

The motto, inspired by Myles Munroe, "Rob the grave and give the world everything you have inside. Die empty," does not just serve as inspirational words for him; it is a way of life, which he embraces wholeheartedly. I am truly honored to stand by Chad's side. My husband's journey is a testament to his character, his determination, and his unwavering commitment to leaving a lasting legacy of purpose and significance.

My prayer is that the words on these pages profoundly affect your life and unlock your full potential to live out the life you desire.

1

Good Intentions vs Intentionally Good

What is the difference between having *good intentions* and being *intentionally good*? In my experience, people often mistake these phrases as the same thing. However, there is a world of difference between the two.

WHAT IT MEANS TO BE INTENTIONALLY GOOD

People want you to judge them by their intentions alone, but I ask you, is that enough? Let's think about that in our own lives for a moment. Imagine working with someone who says he or she will do something but never follows through. Is that enough? Of course not. Saying you'll do something is admirable, but being intentionally good is what brings about real change, because it's aligned with intentional action. We often judge *ourselves* by our intentions, while we judge *others* by their actions. This is the difference between good intentions and intentionally good.

What we actually do, as in what gets accomplished, starts with an intentional approach to each and every day. People often overestimate what they can accomplish in a day and underestimate what they can achieve in their career or lifetime. By placing so much value on the day, we tend to neglect the importance of the process. A habitual process, however, consistently performed over a long period of time, will have a lasting impact.

Habits have a cumulative effect on our lives and ultimately shape our destiny. In his book *Atomic Habits: An Easy & Proven Way to Build Good Habits & Break Bad Ones*, James Clear makes this point through a study on exercise. During 2001, researchers in Great Britain worked with 248 people to build better exercise habits over the course of two weeks. The subjects were divided into three groups.

- **Group 1:** This was the control group. They were asked to track how often they exercised. That's it.
- **Group 2:** This was the "motivation" group. They were asked not only to track their workouts but also to read motivational material on the benefits of exercise.

- **Group 3:** I'll call this the "intentional" group. These subjects received the same presentation as the second group. However, the difference was they were also asked to create a plan for when and where they would exercise by date, time, and location. Here's an example: *"On Wednesday [DATE] at 9:00 a.m. [TIME], I will exercise at the gym on Main Street [LOCATION]."*

The results of the study were surprising. In the first group, 35 percent of people exercised at least once per week, while the second group performed slightly better at 38 percent. Motivation marginally impacted behavior. However, 91 percent of the third group exercised at least once per week when intention was added. By simply specifying date, time, and location, the results more than doubled the normal participation rate.[1]

These results underscore a major difference between *motivation* and *transformation*. *Motivation* is a driving force that compels one to act. But *transformation*—the process of becoming something different—puts action behind intention. I call this formula *time blocking*. Intentionally good people use it every day, and so can you.

> *People often overestimate what can be accomplished in a day and underestimate what can be achieved in their career or lifetime.*

IT'S ABOUT ACTION

Imagine there are five frogs on a log. Four decide to jump off. How many are left? When I ask this question to groups of leaders, I get varying answers. A lot of them say things like, "There's only one," or "You're tricking me." The truth is, there are still five frogs on that log. Each frog *decided* to jump, but none put any action behind it. This merely represents intention—what one intends to do, bring about, or have as a purpose or goal. But intention is nothing without action.

In a *Harvard Business Review* article titled "Strategic Intent," C. K. Prahalad and Gary Hamel highlight the journey of Honda Motor Company's humble beginnings in the 1970s to one of the premier global players in the automobile industry today. What enabled Honda to grow from a small, private Japanese company to a worldwide player? A steadfast strategy of building its business model over the long run, even when it meant forgoing short-term gains. Honda built core competencies and aligned to particular markets others had yet to serve. The company flew under the radar for years, representing no threat to the competition because its focus was different. While everyone else had good intentions and short-term results in mind, Honda was being intentionally good, investing for the long haul to become a major player in the auto industry.[2]

GOOD INTENTIONS VS INTENTIONALLY GOOD

Think about the word *intention* for a moment. To have intent is to have in mind a purpose or a goal. Let's relate that to *intentionally good*. In the case of Honda, there was great clarity around its purpose or goal. However, there's a key difference: intention was backed by action—intentionally good. That's what makes Honda's story different from that of the four frogs with good intentions of jumping off the log.

Let's translate that to you. Intentionally good people— people who have a purpose and a goal of what they want to accomplish—determine the date, time, and location in everything they do. They time block, making room for positive outcomes. I encourage you to apply this to every area of your life. Time block for the gym, your marriage, important deliverables, and so on. Start looking at everything you do through this lens. When you time block, you put action behind good intentions, increasing your chances of succeeding. Time blocking requires discipline, but it's well worth it.

Highly disciplined, intentionally good individuals outperform others—day in and day out.

It boils down to one simple statement: more often than not, highly disciplined, intentionally good individuals outperform others—day in and day out.

What will living an intentionally good life look like? My friend and mentor John Maxwell, who's impacted my life tremendously, answers this question. In his book *Intentional Living*, he pinpoints the differences between good intentions, good actions, and intentionally good.[3] Here are a few examples that you may relate to:

Desire, Action, Results

- Good intentions say *desire.*
- Good actions say *action.*
- Intentionally good says *results.*

Desire is "I want," action is "I do," and result is "I am." I don't desire *to be intentionally good; I* am *intentionally good.*

Someday, Today, Every Day

- Good intentions say *someday.*
- Good actions say *today.*
- Intentionally good says *every day.*

Someday is a maybe, today is the present moment, and every day is perpetual—I show up every day, I improve every day, I make a difference every day.

Fantasy, Strategy, Intentionality

- Good intentions are a *fantasy.*
- Good actions are a *strategy.*

- Intentionally good is *intentionality*.

A fantasy is a dream, a strategy is a game plan, and intentionality brings a dream into reality.

Occasional, Continual, Habitual

- Good intentions are *occasional*.
- Good actions are *continual*.
- Intentionally good is *habitual*.

Occasional is sometimes, continual happens repeatedly with effort, and habitual is a long-standing routine—it's automatic, like brushing your teeth in the morning.

Anyone can do things well occasionally, while fewer can do things continually. But those who commit to habitual routines can become exceptionally high performers all the time.

Based on Emotion, Based on Discipline, Based on a Lifestyle

- Good intentions are based on *emotion*.
- Good actions are based on *discipline*.
- Intentionally good is based on a *lifestyle*.

Based on emotion is sentiment, based on discipline is a set of rules as needed, and based on a lifestyle is a consistent pattern of behavior, habits, and choices that defines one's life—I know who I am and what I want to represent.

Survival, Success, Significance

- Good intentions are about *survival.*
- Good actions are about a life of *success.*
- Intentionally good is about a life of *significance.*

Survival is meeting the minimum standard, success is achieving personal goals, and significance is making a difference in the lives of others. For me, it's about leaving a legacy that impacts future generations.

The examples of Lifestyle and Significance really resonate with me. I learned the lifestyle lesson in 2006, when I was away with my good friend Jake, celebrating his bachelor party. We were staying in a hotel, where I saw a man dressed in a Captain Morgan outfit promoting his company. There was something about the way he carried himself that I found intriguing. It was almost as if he were floating on air as he strolled by me. I couldn't resist commenting to him, "I love the costume."

> Significance is making a difference in the lives of others.

He turned around and replied, "It's not a costume, my friend. It's a lifestyle."

That statement made a lasting impact on me. Too often when it comes to leadership, people treat it as a costume, something they put on for show when they're in the presence of others. But true leadership is not a show; it's a way of living. It's about making the intentional choice not just when we're in the public eye but at all times—acting as a good leader regardless of whose company we are in. That man's words have stayed with me all these years.

This leads me to significance. This is what truly sets apart the extraordinary from the ordinary. Personally, the difference between success and significance is clear: success is all about *me*, but significance is about *others*. Significance is about releasing potential in others, enabling them to positively influence their world. Personally, this is what my wife and business partner, Danielle, and I strive to do in our lives every day. Because in the end, it's not just about survival or success; it's about intentionally creating a lifestyle that leaves a legacy of significance.

> *True leadership is not a show; it's a way of living.*

GETTING TO INTENTIONALLY GOOD

So far, we've gone through what intentionally good looks like in your life. At this point, you may be wondering, *How can I be intentionally good?* Let me share five simple yet powerful steps you can immediately take to awaken your potential.

Step 1–Start Small, Believe Big

Doing anything of significance requires sufficient lead time to build momentum. When you reflect on where you are, especially if you're fairly new to your career, it's important to keep this in mind. If you not only dream big but also believe you have to start big, then you may never take action. You end up hesitant to start because the task at hand becomes too big. For example, starting big may mean you need more resources, time, money, and connections than you currently have. Let's avoid this line of thinking. Instead, let's start small and believe big. Give yourself enough lead time to build up momentum.

A good friend of mine, Waikiki, once helped put this in perspective for me. One day in 2010, he asked, "Chad, tell me your dream."

I replied, "To build a not-for-profit organization that would one day positively influence millions of youth."

He followed up by asking, "What do you need to start it?"

My mind took a straight-line path to starting big. "I need about $30 million. The organization will need a big headquarters and satellite facilities, as well as staff and resources . . ."

Waikiki paused to process my response and then shared a story that epitomized starting small and believing big. He said, "Chad, let me share a story that impacted me." Here's the story he shared:

A young boy was walking on the beach with his father when they spotted some starfish washed up along the shore. The boy ran to the shoreline, picked up one of the starfish, and threw it into the water. He did the same for another starfish, then another one and another one. He repeated this for as many starfish as he saw.

An older gentleman, also walking on the beach, passed the boy and said, "Hey, kid, what are you doing? You think you're making a difference? Look at how many starfish there are!"

The boy walked back to his father, dejected. The father asked, "What happened?"

He said, "That old man made so much sense."

The boy and his father continued walking. As the boy saw more starfish along the shoreline, he decided to throw them back into the water, one by one. The same old gentleman appeared again and said, "Hey, kid, didn't you learn the first time I saw you? You think you're making a difference?"

Pointing in the direction of each starfish he threw back, the boy looked at the old man and said, "Maybe you're right. But I made a difference in this one's life, and I made a difference in this one's life, and I made a difference in this one's life . . ."[4]

This is what starting small and believing big looks like. Get started. Helping the starfish find their way back into the ocean makes a difference, even if it's just one at a time.

It makes a difference to get started. As Andy Stanley says, "Do for one what you wish you could do for everyone."

Step 2—Start Walking, and Your Vision Will Become Clearer

In the story Waikiki shared, as the boy kept walking, everything became clear for him. This is step two—start walking, and your vision will become clearer. As J. P. Morgan, founder of JPMorgan Chase & Co., famously said, "Go as far as you can see; when you get there, you'll be able to see farther."

Reflect on that for a moment. Many times, we want to see the whole picture before we're willing to start walking. Wanting to know every step of the journey is natural. I know that feeling because I've done it myself. But if you want to become intentionally good, simply start walking. Begin with what you have and where you are. If you do this well, it will make all the difference in the world. As you start walking and getting some wins under your belt, momentum builds. Success typically follows. Then you start walking more and advance further. With each step, you gain greater clarity for your vision.

I want to encourage you in your career, wherever you are—whether you're the owner of a business, just starting in an industry, or moving forward in a specific field—start walking and keep walking. Don't stop.

Step 3—Start from Your Area of Giftedness

One of the ways you can be intentionally good is by operating from your area of strength, something we will refer to throughout this book as *giftedness*. We live in a world that tells us to work on our weaknesses. However, I have a powerful message for you: no matter how much you improve in an area of weakness, you'll never go as far as you could if you'd started in your giftedness. This is because no one pays for weaknesses. You will never

> No matter how much you improve in an area of weakness, you'll never go as far as you could if you'd started in your giftedness.

hear anyone say they want to hire an average financial advisor, dine at a mediocre restaurant, have an average marriage, or build an average company. The market will pay a premium for your gifts and can be unforgiving toward weaknesses. It's that simple. Start from your giftedness.

In your area of weakness, you start at poor and the best you'll ever get is average. But in your area of giftedness, you start at average (and in some cases better than average), with the ability to become excellent. The rate of improvement in an area of giftedness is also likely to be very high, giving you a competitive advantage.

Personally, starting from an area of weakness was painful for me. When I tried to improve my weaknesses instead of my giftedness, I often wondered why I was not advancing or growing as fast as I wanted to. I now know why, and hopefully you can benefit from my experience and avoid making the same mistake.

What is giftedness? It's three things: *mission*, *competency*, and *style*. We will reference these many times over, so they're worth explaining in greater detail.

Mission = What You're Passionate About (Your Why)
Competency = What You're Good At (Your What)
Style = How You and Others Perceive You (Your How)

As you get ahead in your career and life, identifying and then operating in your area of giftedness will be key. And when you lead people, make sure you identify and build a team that operates in its area of giftedness. At Lions Pride Leadership, we call this a *gifted organization*. An organization operating in its strengths, a *gifted organization*, is hard to compete with. This is because conventional wisdom tells us to improve on weaknesses.

An organization operating in its strengths, a gifted organization, is hard to compete with.

You can identify your giftedness through observation—but observation can be skewed based on *perspective*, the window through which you see the world, as well as *perception*, the framework used to interpret what you see. I am a strong advocate of using science and technology to help not only identify but also develop your area of giftedness. This can also save you invaluable time. For these reasons, my companies leverage an online leadership assessment to identify an individual's strengths. Observation is good, but when paired with helpful tools, you can more accurately pinpoint and work in your area of giftedness. I encourage you to do the same.

As a person of faith, I also believe operating in your area of giftedness releases the potential within you. Someone's gift will open doors and put him or her in the presence of influential people. It's the gift that does the work, not the person. So many people overvalue the person and undervalue the gift that person possesses. But let me encourage you in this. Begin a lifelong journey where you get better in your area of giftedness every day. The world needs what you have to offer. Do what you were designed to do.

Step 4—Build an Intentional Game Plan

Good intentions—wanting a better life, business, career, family, and so on—are never enough alone. That is simply wishful thinking. However, intentionally good puts action behind the intention. Don't just wish on your intentions; act on them with a game plan for growth.

There are two important elements of the game plan: the *what* and the *how*—*what* to focus on and *how* to go about doing it. Let's start with the *what*.

I want to be intentionally good in five key areas of life, and you'll see this again later in the book. I call them FISHS: financial, intellectual, social, human, and spiritual:

1. *Financial capital*: This is all about your financial assets, including stocks, bonds, real estate, retirement accounts, business interests, and so on.

2. *Intellectual capital*: This is about growing your knowledge base or intelligence quotient (IQ). This could include books you read, podcasts you listen to, and courses you take.

3. *Social capital*: This refers to your relationships and network, alongside how you add value to and/or develop those around you.

4. *Human capital*: Human capital is all about what you bring to the world, including your leadership abilities, giftedness, physical health, and so on.

5. *Spiritual*: Spiritual in this context refers to the values you live by and the traditions that define who you are. These do not have to be religious; rather, your belief systems are core to who you are.

For me, the common denominator is my walk with God. This certainly does not need to apply to you, but part of my walk includes showing people how much I care. As Maya Angelou said, "I've learned that people will forget what you said, people will forget what you did, but people will never forget how you made them feel." So I apply this to all areas of FISHS. It's relevant to my mentors and mentees who help me develop in all five of these areas.

You can get ahead in life by intentionally developing in these areas. I know this firsthand. At the age of twenty-three, I looked in the mirror and didn't like the man I had become. It was during this time that I started on my journey of becoming a lifelong learner. Intentional growth is a game changer because everything you want in life is just on the other side of your personal development.

Now, let's now cover the *how*—*how to go about it*. To intentionally create a growth plan, start today by breaking your life down into phases. Let's take a year of your life. As each game in sports is important to win, so are the twelve months in each year. To win each month, you need to break it into weeks, days, hours, and so on.

This is the key. The world we live in today says *instant gratification*. Culture embraces a microwave nation—thirty seconds, and your food is done. One click, and you have a delivery within twenty-four hours. But *instant* is not how you get ahead in life; that's not success. Real success takes time, breaking a big picture down into smaller pieces. That's the *how* part. Instead of overestimating what you can get done in a day, approach things from what can be achieved over time, in this instance a year.

If you want to have a great year, make sure you have twelve great months. And if you want to have a great month, make sure you have four great weeks. And if you want to have a great week, make sure you have seven great days. And if you want to have a great day, make sure you have twenty-four great hours. Manage every minute. When you manage your minutes, you don't have to worry about your life and career. Your months are going to get better, your years are going to get better, and your life is going to get better. Manage your minutes and watch what happens.

To intentionally create a growth plan, start today by breaking your life down into phases.

Step 5—Begin the Journey of Becoming a Lifelong Learner

Becoming a lifelong learner, developing every day, is one of the most important things I do. That's because in life, we're either moving forward or moving backward. There is no such thing as standing still. The moment we stop growing, we start to atrophy. Individuals who otherwise think they can coast in life are lying to themselves. However, when we're growing, we are becoming the person we want to be. We are being intentionally good. It's not only exciting, but it's also well within your reach. Here are five simple things you can start adding to your daily routine:

1. *Read one book per month in your area of giftedness.*
   Whether you prefer a physical copy or an audiobook, doing this will expand your knowledge and refine your skills. And when you refine your skills, you become more valuable. For example, crude oil is valuable when it comes out of the ground, but it gets even more valuable when you refine it. As you go through your own refining process, growing in your giftedness, your value will also increase. That value is far-reaching—to your family, your company, your community, and so on.

2. *Begin a daily power hour.*
   Why is a daily power hour important? Starting your morning with the right mindset paves the way for the rest of your day. It allows you to get your mind right. It allows space for you to get focused and prepared to take on and conquer the day.

   The better your daily routine, the better results you will have in your life. Good days compound into good weeks, and good weeks turn into good months and years. Before you know it, things add up to a lifetime of success and significance.

It's easy to start. Begin your day with a powerful message or vision to focus on, book to read, or podcast to listen to. For me, I'll read the Bible. This makes all the difference in my day. So be intentionally good and start your daily power hour.

3. *Complete your daily game planner.*
Since 2009, I have been planning each workday in advance of the next. It has become an automatic behavior, like brushing my teeth. Even if I happen to fall asleep before bed, I'll wake up to complete my daily planner. Sometimes, it's my own conscience that will wake me, whereas other times it might be Danielle who provides the nudge. She recognizes how important this is. There are no exceptions—it is a habit that has served me well.

You can start simply, with a blank piece of paper. Here's what mine looks like: I divide the paper into four sections or quadrants. The top left is my calendar for tomorrow. The top right is for priorities that I need to get done that day. The bottom left is for the lessons I learned from the previous day. The bottom right is a running list of all task items. The paper helps me take inventory of what's happening in my life. It all fits on one side of the page. That's the first part.

The second part is something I've found even more powerful: flipping the paper over and using the blank side for note-taking throughout the day. I don't write notes anywhere else—no blackboards, sticky notes, random loose papers, etc. This keeps me from wasting time later looking for where I jotted down a note when I need that information.

If I'm going to be intentionally good, why not maximize my minutes wherever possible? I encourage you to do the same thing using a piece of paper. If you prefer technology, use a device such as the Notes app on an iPad. Whatever you use, complete your daily planner every day.

4. *Document lessons learned from today.*

I once had a wise coach many years ago who warned, "If you don't learn the lesson, it will be repeated—and every repetition will be more painful than the last." A lesson that is not learned repeats again and hurts more. To avoid this, I make a point of documenting my lessons learned each day. I want to avoid the same failure tomorrow that I had today. This is a sign of maturity in one's life; an immature person will repeat problems and failures time and time again, but a mature person learns and adapts.

To put this in perspective, there's a simple yet effective formula I learned personally from John Maxwell. The cycle of success is simply the following:

Test—Fail—Learn—Improve—Reenter

I follow this cycle every day. Documenting the lesson learned puts you in position to improve and reenter. Now imagine if you did that every day of your life. That's an easy-to-repeat refining process. Test something. If it fails, learn from it, document what you learned, and get back in the game tomorrow.

5. *Repeat daily.*

Let's return to where we started this chapter. As I've mentioned, people often overestimate what can be accomplished in a day and underestimate what can be achieved in a career or a lifetime. We generally trick ourselves into thinking we're better than we are, while at the same time we avoid committing to a lifetime of work—in this case, personal development. The hardest person to lead is yourself. But if you can lead yourself well, you've earned the opportunity to lead others. If you can't lead yourself well, why should others trust you with leading them? That's the thing about leadership: it starts with you. The best way to lead yourself well is to choose to be intentionally good and repeat it daily.

Danielle often jokes that I'm asleep as soon as my head hits the pillow at bedtime. That's because

I put actions behind my intentions, and I repeat that process daily. I don't sit up at night wondering what more I could have done each day, because I go to bed empty. Intentionally good means I gave everything I had that day. Living this way will bring you great peace of mind as well. When you go to bed every night, you'll take comfort in knowing you gave everything you had that day.

INTENTIONALLY GOOD IS A PATH TO GREATNESS

We all have greatness inside us. But true greatness is not about doing something extraordinary or out of this world; it's about maximizing our inner potential. Consider a car with a ten-gallon tank cruising city blocks or a 737 jetliner soaring across continents—they're both examples of greatness when their capacity is fully maximized.

You don't need your name in lights for all to see to be considered great. You simply need to reach your potential. The cycle of success is the formula that will help you get there. Don't settle for mediocrity. Now is the time to put action behind intention and strive for excellence in all that you do—let's move forward together by choosing to be intentionally good.

Remember, the difference between good intentions and intentionally good is *action*.

2

We Must Value People to Add Value to People

How can you make the greatest impact on someone's life? It's simple: by valuing them. If we don't *value* people, how could we *add value* to them? All too often in the world today, people are fighting and tearing each other down because they don't see the value in one another. But we have a choice. Right now, we can make a conscious decision to value others. It's not just the right thing to do; it is also the smart thing to do.

A LIFESTYLE CHOICE

It's natural to want everything to revolve around us. But if we are going to truly value others, we must shift our focus to those around us. One of the best examples of valuing others comes from Girl Scouts of the USA, whose mission is to build "courage, confidence, and character" in young girls. Here's an excerpt from their website that tells about Lois Hirschman, a former Girl Scout:

> It was 1938, in the midst of the Great Depression. Lois ("Lofi") Hirschman, now 89 years old, was just 10. Times were tough, and she was struggling with various learning disabilities. The school was another challenge; in those days, students with special needs had little support. Then a friend introduced Lofi to Girl Scouts, and *everything* changed. It was, in her words, "magic."
>
> "Girl Scouting was so good for me as a child. It was the first place I ever got positive feedback," Lofi explained. "The program is written in such a way that you can understand it at any age. It helps you understand where your abilities lie, get good feedback, keep at it, and find a way to do things that work for you. . . .
>
> "I think it's so important to learn to be nice to someone even if you don't want to," she said. "To smile. To help one another. Just simple things. They matter. I think the most beneficial thing about Girl Scouts is the feeling of belonging that you get. The moral code that you learn to actually live by in a way you can understand. . . ."

"There's a magic about Girl Scouts, and that magic is what *every* girl needs," she expressed.[5]

I'd expand on Lofi's story by saying the magic of the Girl Scouts is *what everyone needs*. The magic lies in valuing others—from giving positive feedback to simply being kind. It's a moral code that says to the other person, "You matter to me." This is what makes Girl Scouts successful. In the United States, Girl Scouts started in 1912 with founder Juliette Gordon Low making a difference in the lives of eighteen girls. Fast forward 110 years, and Girl Scouts' influence has spread to 250 million-plus girls globally, and the organization is building a better world through service to others. It started with Juliette first making a lifestyle choice to value people. She then supported that through the creation of Girl Scouts in America.

> "It's so important to learn to be nice to someone even if you don't want to."
> —Lois "Lofi" Hirschman

YOUR ROLE IN VALUING OTHERS

If you value people, you'll add value to them. That is what Juliette Gordon Low did. She valued those girls who grew up in Girl Scouts and, as a result, was able to influence their lives. The interesting thing about Girl Scouts is how wide the impact was—Juliette's small group in 1912 was able to add value to girls such as Lofi, who in turn added value to others. Adding value has a ripple effect, just like a stone dropped in the water. And the more value you add to others, the greater the ripple.

The story of Girl Scouts resonates with me so much given our present day. The world we live in today chases power and influence. You may not realize it, but you probably have some degree of this in your life already. Professionally, you might be working in a flat organization as an employee or in a hierarchical one as a team leader or manager. But regardless of size or shape, we all likely have some impact on others.

It's easy to assert power and influence to get immediate results, but the true measure of a person's character is how they use their power and influence. Pushing one's control may result in short-term results but long-term resentment and animosity. However, deciding to instead serve people when in a position of power and influence is a game changer—one that has the ability to transform lives and organizations. Consider the following:

- According to Officevibe, 69 percent of employees say they would work harder if they felt their efforts were better recognized. Seventy-eight percent said being recognized motivates them in their jobs. Lastly, 72 percent get praise less than once a week.[6]

- *Forbes* reported that employees who feel their voices are heard are 4.6 times more likely to feel empowered to perform their best work.[7]
- And the *New York Times* reports employees who find passion and purpose at work are more than three times as likely to stay with their organizations as those who don't.[8]

These numbers, all powerful, are connected to the value companies place on people. I speak from experience in saying adding value to others changes everything. People work harder because they're motivated to do so. Adding value to them gives them a seat at the table, providing fulfillment in the work they do. They more easily find passion and purpose when they're valued. Whether you're the leader of a company or someone trying to grow in an organization, start adding value to people today so you can realize the return tomorrow.

START WITH AN UNDERSTANDING

To effectively start adding value to others, we must first understand what they want. Despite many influences, there are four core "wants" of people that drive behavior.

#1–*Every person wants to be valued.*

If people have air in their lungs, then they want to be valued. It's a basic human need that gives them a sense of purpose through general recognition. It says, "You matter." Great leaders will make sure people know they are valued.

Personally, the two things I consistently review to show I am valuing people are my calendar and my checkbook. These show me how I am investing my time and where I am allocating my money—and therefore what I value.

#2–*Every person wants to be appreciated.*

What is appreciation? The recognition and enjoyment of someone or something's good qualities. It says, "Thank you so much" for something. When you have appreciation for someone, it's usually because of something good about them, such as qualities you value. Appreciation is encouraging. It brings out more of those qualities in a person.

I personally believe every person is created in God's image. Therefore, I show people appreciation regardless of what they can do for me; it's more about recognition for what God has done for me.

#3—Every person wants to be respected.

As Aretha Franklin sang in her 1967 hit song, "Respect," respect is "What you want . . . What you need." The words to the song literally spell out *respect* as a basic want people are asking for. And it doesn't take much; "just a little bit," as the song says. Respect is a basic requirement that says, "I honor you."

There's a powerful acronym for respect from the Center for Health Professions, University of California, San Francisco. It's called the RESPECT Model, and I've adapted it below for the purposes of this book:

- *Rapport*: to connect on a social level
- *Empathy*: to acknowledge, relate to, and understand
- *Support*: to help overcome barriers
- *Partnership*: to work together
- *Explanation*: to help clarify and understand
- *Competence*: to develop expertise
- *Trust*: to rely on and empower[9]

Just as Aretha Franklin's song says, find out what respect means to people—in your life, business, family, and the like—by demonstrating the above.

#4—*Every person wants to be understood.*

Understanding others requires practicing active listening with an open mind, asking good questions, and putting aside your own agenda. It says, "I get you," or, "I empathize with you." How many times have you been in a conversation in which you're focused on what *you* want to say rather than on listening to the other person?

Communication is not only hearing the words someone is saying but also the tone and intentionality in his or her delivery. You miss this when you're focused on your own agenda, which can include what you're going to say to sound smart to the other person. But if you want to elevate yourself and others, wait and ask smart questions instead.

Understanding requires full engagement with little distractions. Think about the world we live in: the smartphone is the chairman of the board. It controls most aspects of life for most people. The best way to fully engage is to put aside the distractions, including the phone. Look into someone's eyes and be fully present in conversation. This is the best way we can give people all we have. It will help you hear more, understand more, and connect more with others.

People matter. There is no greater capital available than human capital.

I love when business leaders say to me, "I would grow this company more if I didn't have to deal with the people." The truth is, if those same leaders didn't have to "deal" with the people, there would be no company. The bottom line? People matter. There is no greater capital available than human capital. If you understand and focus on what people want, they will help bring success to you and your organization.

HOW TO ADD VALUE IN FOUR STEPS

With an understanding of what people want, let's now jump into action. Here are four core steps you can start taking today to add value to others.

Step 1—Think less about yourself and more about others.

This is such a tough one for so many of us. Let's be honest: it's natural to be focused on yourself. For example, when people show you a picture, who do you look at first? It's you, always. You wonder, *Do I look good?* It's rarely about whether others look good, right? We live in an "I" focused world. But remember what we saw earlier: with only one exception, the world is composed of others. You cannot add value to people without shifting focus to them. Taking the focus off yourself opens your heart and mind to adding value to others.

I make it a practice of adding more value to people than I receive, and I try my best to apply this to every area of my life. This has created great surplus, because those around me reach their full potential. Remember the *gifted organization*? Part of adding value to others in my business endeavors has been about revealing the possibilities in their lives. By valuing them, I've been able to empower them to take action in their area of giftedness to reach their full potential.

Immature leaders focus on themselves while mature leaders focus on others. By adopting this selfless approach, you can empower those around you to reach their potential, creating a surplus that far exceeds your individual success.

Step 2—Practice the Golden Rule.

The golden rule is, "Treat others as you would like to be treated." Now, sometimes I ask others *not* to treat me as they would like to be treated since they don't treat themselves well! But for most people, that is not the case.

Treating oneself well includes managing the feedback loop of our thoughts, beliefs, and behaviors. I am a big believer that your thoughts influence your belief systems, your belief systems affect your behavior, and your behavior creates your results. If we want to see positive change, it's not enough to simply change our behaviors or the outcomes we're seeing.

Above all else, first focus on changing your thought life and belief system, for everything you do flows from them. Start with the thought of adding value to people—*what* you think about. Follow with awareness and belief that "we must value people to add value to people." And reflect on *why* you believe that statement. If our thought life does not align with our belief system, we will never truly add value to others. And finally, our behaviors define *how* we add value—we search for what others value, where they are looking to go in life, and how we can help them. Here's an example, using Lofi Hirschman's Girl Scouts story:

- Thought: *As a lifelong Girl Scout, I know the incredible value I can (will) add to the lives of young girls.*
- Belief: *I believe in my role of developing confidence, leadership skills, and a love for learning in every Girl Scout I encounter.*
- Behavior: *I volunteer my time, supporting the organization through participation and encouraging others with the story of my own experience.*

Your actions, which will create results, start with the thought and belief of valuing people. Therefore, I encourage you to embrace the Golden Rule. Treat people the way you want to be treated—think, believe, and behave in alignment with adding value to others.

Step 3—See everyone as a "10."

Let's have a little fun here: Imagine every person you walk by in your life, career, business, and so forth has a number on their forehead ranging from 1 to 10. It's up to you to put the number there.

For some people, you'll say, "I like him" or "I value her" and give a 10. You might rank others a 5, saying, "I don't like her personality" or "He's not very nice."

Now, let's change the lens you're imagining this through—every person is a 10 because we start with valuing them. Do some people hurt us? Yes. Are there others who are rude to us? No doubt about it. But we still value and try to find ways to add value to them. I know this can be a difficult thing to put in action. What has enabled me to place a 10 on everyone is my faith. I value people not for what they have done or could do for me, but rather because I believe they have been built in God's image. That is why I always put a 10 on people.

Step 4—Ask yourself these three questions:

- Do people know I am willing to help them?
- Do people know I care about them?
- Do people know they can trust me?

If you're able to answer these questions in a positive way, I promise it will change your life forever. Let's take a closer look at each one.

Do people know I am willing to help them? It's important to let the people in your life know you want to add value to them and you're willing to help them, whether it is opening a door or stepping out for them.

Do people know I care about them? Don't assume people understand that you care about them. Take time to tell them you care. Doing so encourages and adds value to them.

Do people know they can trust me? This is such a powerful question, because trust can be broken quickly and easily. But do most people understand how trust is actually established? It's not something that just happens overnight. Let's think of trust like a bank account of relationships. There are debits and credits. If you withdraw more than you deposit, the account becomes overdrawn. In real-life practice, this may be okay at your local bank because you can put more money into the account to bring it current. But in relationships, overdrawing is a problem. When you withdraw from the bank account of relationships and there are insufficient funds, trust is lost. And if someone doesn't trust you, you can't possibly help, speak into, or make a difference in their life.

Trust is such a key element in this process of adding value to people that it's our most important question to answer. Having trust, security in another, allows for potential to be released in the lives you're adding value to.

So how do we best build trust? Consider a 2019 *Harvard Business Review* article that summarized trust across three elements: positive relationships (the ability to create connections with other people and groups), good judgment/expertise (requiring one to be well-informed), and consistency (to "walk the walk" and do what you say you will do). The study, based on the assessments of 87,000 leaders, found that these elements contribute most to trust. Being slightly above average (60th percentile or higher) in all three areas has a profound positive effect, whereas just below average (40th percentile or lower) in any one destroys trust.[10]

INTENTIONALLY GOOD IN VALUING PEOPLE

In the previous chapter, you read about moving from good intentions to intentionally good. Let's now make the connection between intentionality and adding value to others. Remember, there's a good reason to do so, as intentionally good puts action behind the intention.

Following the Golden Rule with Intentionality

Adding value to others means first valuing them. But let's face it, people are complicated. Sometimes they may cause you frustration. Each individual has diverse thoughts, beliefs, and behaviors. You may not understand or agree with their thought life and belief system. Likewise, others might not want to hear a different perspective—*your* perspective. This is why we need to be intentionally good in valuing and adding value to others, managing our own thoughts, beliefs, and behaviors.

The greatest results we seek—career advancement, a better marriage, etc.—begin with thoughts and end with people. And depending on where you are on the age spectrum, it can be hard to change hardwired thoughts learned through observation and repetition over a lifetime. Here are a couple of examples to put this in perspective:

You're like tofu. When you put tofu in a pot to cook, it first absorbs whatever seasoning is in the pot. When fully cooked, the tofu loses its absorption qualities. We're much the same up to about the age of ten. We take in and absorb whatever influences are in our pot of life. From the ages of about eleven to thirty, we take on a finished product that looks, tastes, and feels like the seasoning of life. And after age thirty, it becomes much harder to change.

You're like a garage door. From birth to around ten years old, our garage doors are fully open. Whatever is outside will come into your garage of life. But from around age eleven through thirty, the garage door closes halfway. Now it's not as easy for everything to come in. And whatever you let in up to this point influences your capacity in life. This is why being intentionally good is so important, especially as we get older.

When we're younger, we don't have to try hard to be intentional. If we are fortunate enough to be surrounded by good people, there's a higher probability that we'll find early success. But as we get older, we must be more intentional with our time and effort—who we put ourselves around and how we add value to them. To tie this to the discipline of intentionality, it starts with the practice of first valuing people. It takes effort—and more of it as you get older. But if you'll commit to and put action behind the Golden Rule, there's no question you'll achieve your greatest results.

Reaching Your Greatest Results with a Plan

John Maxwell has often shared a story about a question he was asked that changed his life forever: "Do you have a plan for personal growth?" That's the question Curt Kampmeier asked John over breakfast when he was twenty-five years old. Curt was someone John had sought out as a mentor.

Up to this point, John's growth in life had been due to his energy and charisma, with perhaps a little bit of luck and chance in between. After fumbling for an answer, John finally acknowledged that he did not have a plan. That question proved to be a turning point in his life. The rest is history. Now, the very same question posed to John is the one I ask you. Do *you* have a plan for personal growth?

Your greatest results are well within reach. But you have to be intentional, leaving little to luck and chance. Don't drift to success; go there intentionally. Plan how you will add value to others, grow yourself in turn, and achieve results.

Having the Right Attitude

A simple yet powerful piece of advice is to simply be friendly and cheerful. Yes, you read that right. A cheerful attitude toward everyone you speak to can make all the difference in your life.

You may have just started a new job, or perhaps you're looking to get ahead in your current one. Showing up a little bit earlier and giving a little bit more can go a long way. Take two people who are equally competent in the same industry—one is cheerful and friendly while the other is a grouch. Who is more likely to get ahead over time, land the role, get promoted, and earn more? The cheerful and friendly one, of course.

If we are going to add value to people, we need the right attitude. Do everything with excitement and energy to help others and make a difference. Be intentional about it. Those who advance in their careers are the very same people who intentionally add value to others. So invest in people and do it with enthusiasm.

Investing in Others by Setting an Example

The thing about leadership is that people can observe it. A leader's values and behaviors are always on display for others to see. Great leaders go out of their way to also care for others. And exceptional leaders are intentionally good at adding value to others. They take good intentions and back them up with action.

One of the most effective ways I've seen this done is through an observation exercise I require of everyone I mentor. It's an easy-to-follow practice that we'll cover more in-depth in later chapters.

Step 1: I do something (the performance of a task or activity). I do the work. How easy is that?

Step 2: I do it, and now someone is next to me. Now, I'm starting to add value to people.

Step 3: They do it, and I'm next to them. I observe and provide good feedback, and it's of greater value to them.

Step 4: They can do it—the value I've added to them has been fulfilled.

Step 5: I take the person who I had next to me and put a new person next to them and repeat the five steps. This multiplies the impact I have, making a major difference in more people's lives.

If you want to get something done quickly, do it yourself, sure. A lot of people think, *Let me do me, and you do you.* But the truth is, we need others. This is why we've emphasized valuing people to add value to them. If you want to go far, bring others along with you for the journey and watch your impact multiply.

Making a Lifestyle Choice

As I've said, valuing people is a lifestyle choice. If you've had a lifestyle of not needing others, I want to challenge that line of thinking by illustrating a few business models in practice today.

- *Business Model 1—Codependence*
  Two or more entities become excessively reliant on one another. The individual success of one is tied

to the other's existence. It's a "needy" model where negative behaviors or actions may be enabled in order to maintain the relationship. Codependency is not a healthy relationship, especially in a business relationship or a leadership function.

- *Business Model 2—Independence*
A business or entity operates on its own in a self-sufficient way that is not dependent on anyone else. This is the "you don't need anyone" or "do it on your own" model. But it's simply not true. The impact is small in the independence model.

- *Business Model 3—Interdependence*
Two or more entities work together to achieve shared objectives. This model says, "I need you, and you need me." We both have different gifts and collectively benefit from one another.

Business model 3 is where mature leaders make a difference and add value to people's lives. How do we add value to people? By working together—that's what it's all about. Unfortunately, we are often taught to focus on ourselves to get to the next level. I challenge you to think differently in your business as well as your personal relationships. Build an interdependent model where I value what you bring, and you value what I bring, to the table. And because we each bring something different, the impact is multiplied.

WE MUST VALUE PEOPLE TO ADD VALUE TO PEOPLE

TAKING THE FIRST STEP

The first time Danielle and I met with John Maxwell for lunch, we gave him a small but memorable gift. We did this before he started mentoring us, working with our company, and speaking into our lives. This was the beginning of a great relationship, a friendship that was forged by both of us stepping out to add value to one another. And it started with someone taking the first step.

As the great Zig Ziglar often said, "You can have everything in life you want, if you will just help other people get what they want." This means you take the first step and add value. If we know from our lessons in this chapter that everyone wants to be valued, why wait in giving them what they want? Take the first step—add value to people. Don't wait for someone to add value to you. Step out as a leader—leaders go first.

Add value to people, and I promise they'll add value to you in return.

A word from the author

3

Make Your Purpose Bigger Than Your Problem

L ife is never made unbearable by circumstances but only by lack of meaning and purpose." This well-known quote is from Viktor Frankl, a man who lived from 1905 to 1997, including during one of the most destructive periods in world history—World War II. Best known for being a Holocaust survivor, Viktor was thirty-seven years old when he entered the concentration camps. He spent three years in four camps and suffered tremendous loss, losing his father, mother, brother, and wife in the Holocaust.

THERE'S PURPOSE IN EVERYTHING

By every metric, Viktor had a very difficult life. However, in spite of the adversity, he made his purpose bigger than his problem. His purpose? A life devoted to psychiatry and neurology, specializing in recognition of meaning as a way of improving mental health.

Prior to and continuing after the war, Viktor's own psychology theory, called *logotherapy* (Greek for "healing"), was an approach to help people find personal meaning in life, despite hardship and suffering. Years later, logotherapy institutes were created around the world, offering training, therapy, and research in meaning-centered psychotherapy. Frankl's experience in concentration camps also led to his most popular book, *Man's Search for Meaning*, originally released in 1946. Sometimes when you read a book, you mark it up. This book happens to be one that marked *me*.

The English translation was published in 1959 and became an international bestseller. In 1991, it was listed "among the ten most influential books in America" by the Library of Congress.[11] To no surprise, it is consistently on Amazon's top 100 books list and is often recommended as one of the top 100 books to read in a lifetime.

Victor Frankl believed that life can have meaning even in the most difficult of circumstances. There's probably no better example of making one's purpose bigger than a problem. Frankl experienced great loss and suffering. But he did not let his problems and tragic losses get in the way of his purpose of helping people find healing through meaning.

PURPOSE VS PROBLEM: IT'S A CHOICE

If your problem gets too big, it covers up your purpose.

Here's an example to illustrate this relationship. Let's say the sun is your purpose and a cloud is your problem. If the cloud is in front of the sun, depending on the cloud's size, you can still see the sun. In the same way, the purpose can be seen through the problem. But what happens if you make that cloud bigger? Just as the cloud will eventually block the sun, so, too, will your purpose become hidden by the problem. Now you can't see your purpose through your problem.

This is what most people do. Whether they realize it or not, people are actually making a choice about the size of the problem. They choose to make the problem bigger than the purpose. We all certainly face different challenges that can feel overwhelming—financial struggles, a bad health diagnosis, relationship issues, addiction, the loss of loved ones, and so on. It's so easy to get consumed with the problem. But when we choose the purpose over the problem, we are able to see through the problem.

As T. D. Jakes has said, "If you can't figure out your purpose, figure out your passion. For your passion will lead you right into your purpose." Your purpose, just like the sun, can be an incredibly bright and intense force in your life. If you have a burning passion for it, there's no problem that can overshadow it.

Don't let your problem get too big; choose your purpose and harness its power. If you do this, it will shine through any problem, just as the sun can shine through any cloud.

As a leader and lifelong learner, I've analyzed the lives of great leaders. The one thing that stands out is that anyone who achieved success faced obstacles and problems. The difference maker in each? Any great leader throughout history—military officers, great men and women of the Bible, presidents—made their purpose bigger than their problem.

Take Nelson Mandela, for example. He spent almost three decades in prison for his activism yet never lost sight of his purpose—to end apartheid in South Africa. Or Abraham Lincoln, who faced a bloody civil war during his presidency but stayed true to his purpose—to preserve the Union and abolish slavery. In each example, the purpose prevailed because it was big. What would have been the impact if they instead chose to make the problem bigger?

When I look at my personal life, some of the biggest struggles resulted in the greatest things Danielle and I have achieved. Our biggest professional struggles were a bad business deal and a relationship gone south. I recall how devastating they were to us. It was then that we realized there was a choice to be made between purpose and problem. We decided (and often reminded each other), "The problem's big, but we're going to make our purpose bigger." From there, we birthed two organizations: our coaching company, Lions Pride Leadership, and our non-profit, I AM Empowering. If you make your purpose bigger than your problem, I can promise you this: you are going to succeed. It's not *if* but rather *when*.

We all have the same choice between purpose and problem. As I write this, you may be going through something in your life. I urge you to take a step back and put it in perspective. Your choices matter. Today, right now, you have a choice. I believe there's a greater purpose for any problem in your life.

> *If you make your purpose bigger than your problem, I can promise you this: you are going to succeed.*

Don't lose sight of it. The purpose will provide motivation and push you through difficult times to achieve it. Purpose, when fulfilled, equals success.

THE PURPOSE ECONOMY

The pandemic of 2020 and 2021 changed the perspective of many people. Of course, COVID-19 brought with it a great deal of tragedy and hardship. But even amid these difficulties, there was a silver lining: the pandemic gave many an opportunity to reevaluate priorities and consider what truly matters. It gave people a chance to step back from the rat race and think differently. A new economy emerged, one where people asked themselves, "What do I want to do?" and "What's my meaning?" and "Why am I here?" Consider the following stats for US-based employees from McKinsey & Company.[12]

- Nearly 50 percent of employees said they are reconsidering the kind of work they do because of the pandemic.
- Nearly two-thirds of US-based employees said that COVID-19 has caused them to reflect on their purpose in life.
- Millennials were three times more likely than others to say that they were reevaluating work.

Why do these stats matter? It all adds up to purpose—purpose matters like never before. The title of McKinsey's survey alone says it all: "Help Your Employees Find Purpose—or Watch Them Leave." And while the survey is US-based, it speaks universally to what people care about.

Purpose matters for you, the people you work for, the ones you work with, and anyone who works for you. As I mentioned before, every single person has a purpose. I didn't understand this years ago, but I do today. Great leaders in this new economy not only make purpose bigger than their problem but also help others identify their purpose. And they take it a step further by connecting individual purpose with the organization's purpose. When this happens, it becomes a win-win. As leaders in our own right, we all have the ability to do the same.

PURPOSE & ALIGNMENT

So what is "purpose"? It refers to the reason for which something is done or created or for which something exists. There are two types of purpose:

1. Life and work purpose: *Why do you exist?*
2. Business purpose: *Why does the company exist?*

Great organizations connect both types of purpose. If you can do this well, whether aligning people with business purpose or identifying a company that aligns with your life and work purpose, you're going to win in this new economy. Why? With the rise of the millennials and the upcoming generation, people want their work to matter—to them and to the company.

Let me share an example from my professional life. One of our team members, Ann-Marie, is also a close friend. One day, Ann-Marie and her husband shared her vision with me. She wanted to develop the next generation of leaders so they could positively impact society. I remember immediately running into my office and revealing to her what God revealed to me. In my notebook, I shared with her the vision for our nonprofit, I AM Empowering.

I held out a document, smiled, and said, "Ann-Marie, look!" The document showed a multigenerational vision for empowering youth and transforming public and private school systems.

Ann-Marie responded, "That's my vision too!" At that moment, something happened. She was able to see how she could fulfill her purpose within the organization's purpose, connecting her life's purpose with her business's purpose.

In the new economy, the *purpose* economy, people want to feel valued and connected to their work. It's no longer good enough to just clock in, do the work, and clock out. The purpose economy demands more. People need to connect to what they do.

Think about when a car needs a wheel alignment. Imagine how driving the car feels: shaking and rattling. You might get to where you're going, but it's going to be rough and bumpy. But when you get a wheel alignment, the tires come into balance and the drive

The person we are meant to become should exceed the price paid.

becomes smooth. How much further could you now go? It's the same thing with purpose and alignment; it makes all the difference in the world. Where there's alignment, there's fulfillment. This is where the magic happens between people and organizations.

Years ago, I was coaching an executive on the principles that govern how one of our companies advises clients. It's an intentional methodology we call "Family First Alignment" or "Business Model Alignment." In short, we look to align an individual's life and work by identifying the following: purpose, vision, values, giftedness, and strategy—in that order. One of the things the executive realized was the purpose and vision for her life could never be accomplished at the company she was working at. The reason was the company's purpose and the executive's purpose were out of alignment. This shifted everything for the executive, as she realized a change was needed to fulfill her purpose.

Change can be painful, but in the end the person we are meant to become should exceed the price paid.

THE ROLE OF GIFTEDNESS

One of the top reasons people leave their jobs is because their gifts and talents are not being utilized. If you think this is different from leaving for better pay, think again. When you operate from an area of giftedness, the market will pay a premium for those gifts. When you don't, the opposite happens. It's just that simple.

How does giftedness factor into purpose? Let's return to its definition. Giftedness is three things:

Mission = What You're Passionate About (Your Why)

Competency = What You're Good At (Your What)

Style = How You and Others Perceive You (Your How)

Placing an emphasis on mission, our giftedness aligns to passion. Passion, in turn, leads you to purpose. Great leaders identify organizations or create working environments that are great fits for their mission. When this happens, there's a better chance of operating in one's area of giftedness. As a leader, you, too, can do the same. Build an environment that aligns with people's passions and interests. If you do this, they'll also find their purpose.

> *Giftedness aligns to passion, and passion leads you to purpose.*

HAVE A PURPOSE THAT IS CLEAR

If your purpose is clear, the right people will be attracted to it. Let's take a real-world example in Nordstrom. Founded by John W. Nordstrom and Carl F. Wallin in 1901, the company was built on the premise that customers deserved the best service, selection, quality, and value. Here's an excerpt from the company's website:

At Nordstrom, Inc., we exist to help our customers feel good and look their best. Since starting as a shoe store in 1901, how to best serve customers has been at the center of every decision we make. This heritage of service is the foundation we're building on as we provide convenience and true connection for our customers.[13]

Nordstrom's message is clear. It has since evolved to operate for well over a century. That doesn't happen by accident. Its message—the purpose—has likely attracted people who are passionate about helping others and going the extra mile to create a positive impact. But let's take it one step further.

An immigrant who left Sweden at the age of sixteen, John W. Nordstrom arrived in the United States unable to speak a word of English and with only five dollars in his pocket.[14] Believing success would come only by offering customers the best service, selection, quality, and value, he made this his purpose. It became not only a driving force that shaped what is known as Nordstrom today but also a magnet that attracted like-minded talent.

Have a clear and powerful message that reflects your purpose. You may have people who are repelled by it, but that's okay. I had a coach many years ago who said to me, "Make sure that you have a message that either attracts people or repels people. The worst thing is to be lukewarm in the middle."

Your message should make people say, "Wow, I need to work with this person (or company)." If it doesn't, you're better off repelling them. Here's an example from Lions Pride Leadership:

- **A Clear Purpose:** *We believe the best in people. We exist to awaken, empower, and equip leaders to reach their full potential.*
- **Who It Attracts:** *Individuals with a passion for developing people and who understand the positive impact it has in their world.*
- **Who It Repels:** *Anyone who is self-focused and/or underestimates the impact of self-development and personal growth.*
- **How It Relates to Giftedness:** *Utilizing team members' strengths to create a gifted organization that gives us a competitive advantage.*

Remember, average is the best you can hope for in an area of weakness. Build a gifted organization that has everyone operating in an area of strength. Everyone's strengths are different. What's enjoyable for one may be drudgery for another. But if we are intentional about identifying giftedness and aligning it with common purpose, excellence is inevitable.

STEPS TO FOLLOW

"Make your purpose bigger than your problem" is a powerful statement to live by. So, let's strive to do just that. Following are seven practical steps you can follow, some of which we've already covered but are reinforced here for completeness:

Step 1—Identify Your Giftedness

As we get older, it takes more effort to identify our gifts. But children are a great example for us to follow. Just look at how kids play in a schoolyard. If you watch long enough, each child does what he or she is designed to do. Why? Because children do what they have a passion for, long before the pressures and expectations of the world get in the way. They use what comes naturally to them—their gifts. To that end, we, too, must use our gifts. Our purpose calls for it. Without it, we will become frustrated and might even walk away from something when times get tough.

It comes down to strengths and weaknesses. As a mature leader, I have come to recognize that I get energy in my strength zone and I'm drained in my weakness zone. Therefore, I try to spend as much time as possible in my giftedness. What is giftedness? You'll hear this repeatedly, because it's so important: Mission, competency, and style.

As mentioned in earlier chapters, identifying your giftedness can be done through observation. But if you can use technology to help you, it will save lots of invaluable time. For that reason, I encourage you to check out what we use at Lions Pride Leadership: PRO-D, a leadership self-assessment that gives you answers to who you are and what you do best. It is designed to reveal your giftedness.

Step 2—Identify What You're Willing to Sacrifice to Achieve That Purpose

What are you willing to sacrifice in pursuit of your purpose? That's what step 2 is all about. In John Maxwell's book *The 21 Irrefutable Laws of Leadership*, the "Law of Sacrifice" says it best: "A leader must give up to go up."[15] When John decided to create a digital course of the book, he invited me to teach this law. While preparing for that, I came to realize too many people want success without the effort. Everyone wants to get ahead in life, but not everyone is willing to sacrifice.

Danielle and I have dreams that have been deposited in our hearts for our coaching company to be franchised across one thousand US cities; for our nonprofit, I AM Empowering, to work with the Department of Education and local communities in one thousand US cities; and for our generational planning firm to have offices in twelve cities across the United States. Dreams like that just don't happen on their own. If you want to accomplish any dream, any purpose for your life, you have to become intentionally good about sacrificing things.

Many years ago, we gave up a luxurious condominium in a beautiful building in pursuit of the purpose God gave us. We were blessed to have lived with my mother-in-law for seven years during that time, allowing us to take the resources we had and reinvest them into one of our companies, year after year. We could have done so many other things, but we sacrificed. Even to this day, we sacrifice instead of taking profit where we can, reinvesting back into the company—hiring more people and expanding to other cities across the United States.

Sacrifice is a choice. There's simply a cost to every dream, vision, or purpose. Some people are willing to pay the price, while others are not. There are going to be nights or weekends when we miss time with loved ones. As a case in point, this very sentence was written on a weekend in pursuit of making a difference in your life. We all can make our purpose bigger than our problem, but sometimes we need to sacrifice to achieve it. Don't go on the journey first, then count the cost. Count the cost first, be willing to pay it, and go on the journey thereafter. Here are some examples of sacrifice:

Sacrificing your time: Achieving one's purpose often requires time—nights and weekends as well as time otherwise spent on personal relationships. There may be a night when we have to say to a loved one, "I'm sorry, I can't be there."

Sacrificing material possessions: This is sacrificing luxuries and expensive purchases for investment in your purpose. Think of the example I shared in my life of moving from a luxurious condominium. We may need to downsize our lives to fund our dreams.

Sacrificing profit today for your future vision: We may have the ability at times to earn a higher income or maximize profit in the short term. But we sacrifice and instead reinvest it back into the purpose. For example, Apple reinvested a significant portion of its profits into research and development during the early 2000s to continually innovate and grow. One of the results was the iPhone. Sometimes we have to sacrifice today to maximize tomorrow.

Sacrificing sleeping in: It's easier to stay in bed. But if we are going to make our purpose big, we'll need to maximize every minute of the day. This may mean sacrificing that extra time to rest in the morning. We cannot afford to sleep in on a big purpose.

Sacrificing unhealthy food habits: Unhealthy food habits are convenient but can wreak havoc to any pursuit. Maintaining a healthy diet contributes to a peak physical state, provides mental clarity, and helps us avoid problems that can overshadow our purpose—and that's what this is all about.

Step 3—Create a Personal Growth Plan to Develop Your Area of Giftedness

Up to this point, we've spoken about giftedness at length. But giftedness alone is not enough. How are you going to grow from where you are to where you want to go in life? Create a personal growth plan to develop your area of giftedness. You don't just drift to success; you grow into it. You have the potential. But potential requires development, learning skill sets in your area of strength.

Step 4—Always See a Bigger Purpose through the Problem

Let me share a personal story to reinforce the overarching lesson of this chapter. It was 2006, and I was just starting to see success in my career and life. At this pivotal point in time, my father passed away at the age of fifty-eight. Losing him was hard; I loved him tremendously. It was during this time I decided to live out what God had planted in my heart. I was having a conversation with my older brother, Marc, when I decided to make my purpose bigger than my problem. I told him, "One day, we'll have a foundation in honor of Dad that makes a major difference in this world."

I made a decision right then and there to use my father's death as a motivating factor to fulfill the purpose I had in my heart. Almost two decades later, I find myself living out that purpose. But it could have been very different. Just a change in my choice would have resulted in an entirely different trajectory.

Everyone goes through hardship and pain, but how we respond matters most. No matter what comes, don't let current circumstances negatively affect your future. We all make choices daily. But understand this: *the choices we make* make *us*. That's the difference between maturity and immaturity. Every time a problem comes about, make the mature choice and decide to make your purpose bigger. When you do this, I promise you will always see your purpose through the problem.

> The choices we make make us.

Step 5—Develop an Intentional Family-First or Business Model Alignment

When developing a model to follow for our lives, whether it's for our family or in business, don't just have good intentions. There's an intentionally good approach that takes into account six key principles or pillars for success:

1. **Purpose:** *why you or your business exists*
2. **Vision:** *what success looks like for you, your family, or your business*
3. **Values:** *principles you, your family, or your business lives by*
4. **Giftedness:** *the areas of strength for you, your family members, or your company*
5. **Strategy:** *the plan to accomplish the vision, protect values, and keep people in their giftedness*
6. **Metrics:** *what we use to hold ourselves accountable*

Taking great care across each will generate a high level of intentionality that will enable any hopes, dreams, or vision for your life.

One principle from this list I want to especially highlight is *values*. Danielle and I share the same set of values in both our personal and professional lives. We'll reference and expand on them throughout the book. They go by the acronym LISTENS:

- Lifelong learner
- Intentional
- Stewardship
- Teamwork
- Excellence
- Nonattachment
- Simplicity

Those are our values. The last value, simplicity, was added after eight years. Why? Simplicity is enablement. The more complex something is, the harder it is to manage and be effective with. Complexity breaks down communication, which in turn breaks down trust. But simplicity enables understanding, which ultimately leads to action. Take the complex and make it simpler.

I encourage you to create a family first or business model alignment that incorporates your purpose, vision, values, giftedness, strategy, and metrics. If you go in that order, you will have the ability to always make your purpose bigger than your problem.

Step 6—Integrate Your Team Members' "Life & Work" Purpose with the Business's Purpose

In our old headquarters, Danielle and I had a beautiful office with a view of the parking lot. At around 4:59 p.m. every day, I would see through my window a traffic jam forming by the parking gate. Everyone was fighting to get through at 4:59 p.m., as if the office building were going to disappear at 5:00 p.m. As Yogi Berra once said, "You can observe a lot by just watching." It was clear people were eager to leave.

No matter where you are, if your "outside" is more fun and fulfilling than your "inside," your people inside are going to want to get outside. Said differently, if your company is not helping people fulfill their purpose, the same people will change companies. But what won't change is this one constant: you are always going to have a problem after 5:00 p.m. That's why I teach businesses and individuals alike to make the inside so great that people don't run to get outside. I learned this from my pastor, Joe Mattera, who once said to me, "Families that play together, stay together." Let's relate that to business. Teams that have fun together, stay together.

How do you ensure fun? Integrate team members' life purposes with the business. Remember Ann-Marie's story? She found fulfillment by aligning her purpose with our work. And we have so much fun doing it together. When there's fulfillment,

> *Teams that have fun together, stay together.*

inside is more fun than outside. People come together every day, aligned and excited to do great things.

Step 7—Make It a "Win-Three" or Win-Win-Win

A coach of mine once said, "In everything you do, ask, 'How do I make it a win-three?'" This means: (1) a win for clients, (2) a win for team members, and (3) a win for the business. It's about finding the wins, threefold. But in the world today, most people are fighting against one another to win at all costs. It's "you have to lose, so

I can win" or "if you win, I lose." But it doesn't have to be that way.

Getting a "win-three" starts with collaboration. After all, a strong collaboration divides the work to multiply the impact. Let us consider this for every aspect of life—a strong friendship, marriage, business, or team. When we are aligned toward a common goal, we can achieve far more. Just think of this: one

> *Let purpose be the yoke that pairs us for success.*

ox can pull nine thousand pounds of weight. How much would you guess two oxen can pull? The answer may surprise you: twenty-seven thousand pounds, or three times the amount of one ox alone. What enables this is the yoke— the wooden beam—that pairs the oxen together. The yoke goes around their necks, creating an alignment between the two. Now the oxen can work together effectively.

Similarly, this concept of alignment applies to business. Organizations that have alignment in purpose get multiplication because dividing the work is natural. Here's another example from Lions Pride Leadership:

- **A Win for Our Clients:** *Personalized coaching helps clients (leaders) improve their leadership skills to achieve goals.*
- **A Win for Our Team Members:** *Team members who have a passion for making a difference in the*

lives of others find fulfillment when helping clients reach their goals.

- **A Win for Our Business:** *Utilizing team members' strengths (giftedness) increases the probability of our organization winning.*

We all can make it a "win-three." Let purpose be the yoke that pairs us for success.

SEEING PURPOSE THROUGH ANYTHING

As you move forward in life, problems occur. It's not a matter of *if* but rather *when* they do. No matter the time, make your purpose bigger than the problem. If you do this, you'll always be able to see your purpose through the problem. If you otherwise can't see it, redefine it by asking, "Why do I exist?"

Knowing your purpose and making it bigger than any problem will make all the difference in your personal and work life. That's because the purpose will become a compass that always points you in the right direction, no matter how rough the waters are.

A word from the author

Give More Than You Take

Giving more than you take is a simple philosophy that holds great power. It's a way of looking at life through the lens of abundance. As Jim Rohn once said, "Giving is better than receiving because giving starts the receiving process."

THE GREAT POWER OF GIVING

To illustrate this point, I'd like to share the story of our friend Mark Cole and his relationship with John Maxwell.

As the CEO and owner of the John Maxwell enterprise, Mark Cole has worked more closely with John than anyone else—this includes accompanying him on countless trips to countries all over the world. With decades of leadership experience, there's probably no one more uniquely qualified to play this role. But what is really interesting is how Mark got to this point. He started as a cold caller filling seats for John's events and eventually moved up nine positions to CEO and owner. How did he do it? By giving more than he took.

Mark Cole's efforts helped him separate from the crowd, catching the attention of John Maxwell's assistant Linda and later John himself. Because he consistently stood out from the pack, John eventually met Mark after a few years. He shared a powerful message, telling Mark, "One day, if you want, you could be the owner of this company." But to do so, Mark was told he would have to give more than he takes. He would have to add greater value to the company by developing leaders to take his spot as he climbed to higher levels.

As Mark continually rose to meet that challenge, he was given greater responsibility. Each time, Mark gave more value than he took. And each time, he found greater abundance in his life. As Joel Osteen once said, "When you focus on being a blessing, God makes sure that you are always blessed in abundance." Mark did that in John's life and eventually others' lives, making his life one long gift that has added value to many.

My friend, if there's one message to take from Mark's story, it's this: you have the ability to do the same.

ENGAGEMENT

A foundation to giving more is *engagement*. Staying engaged enables an understanding for what people truly need, allowing us to give more than we take. Engagement, for all intents and purposes, is also a form of giving. It's how Mark Cole climbed the ladder, developing leaders to replace him by giving them his time, attention, and effort. Consider the following statistics from Gallop on higher levels of engagement and the effect on business outcomes:

- 41 percent lower absenteeism: More people show up to work when they are engaged.
- 24 percent lower turnover from higher turnover organizations: Those who are engaged are less likely to leave their jobs, even when others around them are leaving.
- 17 percent higher productivity: An engaged team is more invested in the work and success of the company.
- 21 percent higher profitability: An engaged team works productively to achieve the company's purpose.[16]

Organizations that engage people give more than they take, just as Mark Cole did for John Maxwell's companies. They have greater connections and less turnover. And the team members showing up to work are more productive, driving fulfillment and profitability higher.

We all have the ability to be a Mark Cole and see the same results by giving more to others. So how come there are not more Mark Cole stories? To answer that, consider the struggle between two sides. On one side, the world says, "Don't do it" or "You can't." The other side says, "Of course you can make it happen." As we discussed in the previous chapter, people

> "Effective people are not problem-minded; they're opportunity-minded."
> — Stephen Covey

tend to choose the problem. In this case, they choose the side that says, "You can't," and find the problem to justify *why* they can't. But you don't have to make the same choice.

Stephen Covey said it best: "Effective people are not problem-minded; they're opportunity-minded. They feed opportunities and starve problems."[17] When you starve something, it dies. I encourage you to be opportunity-minded. To give more than we take, choose the side of opportunity and starve the mindset of *can't*. This is choosing an abundant mindset.

ABUNDANCE VS SCARCITY

Let's unpack two different mindsets and their effect on our daily lives: the abundance mindset and the scarcity mindset. Here are a few examples of their influence on people:

Always More vs Never Enough

Abundance says there is plenty to go around, or there's always enough. The pie is expandable, and we can work together.

Scarcity, on the other hand, says this is a zero-sum game. Gains come at the expense of others, and we have to compete.

Happy to Share vs Stingy

Abundance means being generous and willing to share with others. People with an abundance mindset want to share knowledge and make a difference in people's lives— paying it forward or opening doors with connections.

Scarcity is being stingy or reluctant to share. Connections or resources are hoarded, and information may be held back.

Rapport vs Suspicion

Abundance defaults to building rapport and creating relationships, believing the best results come from collaboration. Trust is built early.

However, scarcity defaults to suspicion. It's hard to build relationships with a scarcity mindset. Others may be seen as a threat and fighting may ensue.

Welcomes Competitors vs Resents Competitors

Abundance welcomes competition as a way to grow and improve—competition makes the pie bigger to someone with an abundant mindset. It's where everyone wins, and the success of others is encouraging.

Scarcity, however, resents the competition. With a scarcity mindset, competition is seen as a threat to success because of the belief that the pie is smaller. The view is, it's either me or them. If they're doing it, I can't. It's a limiting belief system.

There's one thing I'd like to emphasize in competition: Abundance is an "and" lifestyle of multiple options rooted in abundance. It's "you *and* me." But "or" is an either/or scenario of limited options rooted in scarcity. That's "you *or* me."

Thankful vs Entitled

Abundance focuses on gratitude. People with an abundant mindset are thankful for the blessings in their lives.

Scarcity focuses on lack. People with a scarcity mindset believe they deserve more than what they have and that people are there to serve them.

Giving More vs Giving Less

Abundance understands the importance of giving more than is expected. People with an abundance mindset ask, "How can I give more than I'm getting paid to do?" And they advance further than people with a scarcity mindset.

Scarcity asks, "How can I get by with doing less than what is expected from me?" It is *giving* as little as possible and *taking* as much as possible.

Thinking Big vs Thinking Small

Abundance thinks the future is brighter than the past. People with an abundance mindset believe great things are achievable and embrace risks to make them happen. They understand calculated risk leads them closer to where they want to go.

Scarcity, however, thinks small and avoids risk. Failure and negative outcomes are feared. Failure is not seen as a friend but rather a foe to avoid at all costs.

Optimistic vs Pessimistic

Abundance believes the best is yet to come, that there's surplus. Things will work out in the end. There are no setbacks or challenges that can't be overcome with an abundance mindset.

Scarcity, however, believes tough times are always ahead. The future is bleak and uncertain. Opportunities may be missed for worry of what could go wrong.

Which of these examples speak to you? Are there any that you sometimes find yourself associating with?

I believe we all, at times, have had a scarcity mindset. I share the following story often. At twenty-three years old, I was living in a basement apartment, unhappy with my life choices. The man I had become associated with scarcity in everything—lacking, insufficient, limited, and avoiding accountability for where I was in life. I finally looked in the mirror one day and made a life choice to have an abundance mindset. That choice began to change the direction of my life.

Now, I'd love to tell you it was as easy as flipping a switch labeled "abundance mindset," but that's not what happened. The old mindset of scarcity did not die easily; it fought for survival, seeping into my mind every day. I compare it to good versus evil; it felt like a competition between two forces. But I was committed to having an abundance mindset. That commitment started with my thoughts and beliefs. And as I discussed earlier, thoughts impact beliefs, beliefs impact behaviors, and behaviors create results.

Years ago, during a difficult time financially with one of our companies, I had a coach tell me, "You're struggling because you don't like selling." The company, at the time, was a traditional life insurance business.

Defensively, I responded, "I love selling."

My coach continued, "No, you don't love selling; you love helping people. This next year, focus on changing the word *selling* to *helping*."

So instead of asking me how many families or businesses I could sell to, he was asking me to think about how many families or businesses I could help. Guess what happened that year? When my thoughts and beliefs changed, so did my behavior—and the results for the company. We saw a 500 percent increase in revenue.

My focus on *selling* reflected a scarcity mindset. I internalized it as, *I have to separate people from their money.* It was "you *or* me." The shift to *helping* reflected an abundance mindset. The narrative was, *What I do helps people with their money.* It was now "you *and* me." The breakthrough catapulted our performance and helped the company evolve into an organization that advises and coaches successful family business owners under the philosophy of Tax Efficient, Legally Minded, and putting Families First.

We can never realize our full potential when we're consumed by negative thoughts and beliefs. Negativity brews a mindset of scarcity. Sometimes those thoughts and beliefs are subtle. For example, here are two simple questions I often ask people:

1. Tell me about your high school days.
2. Tell me what you're doing now or what you want to accomplish.

Are they more excited talking about where they came from, or are they more excited talking about where they're going? This reveals perspective, whether they believe their best days are behind them (scarcity mindset) or the future is bright (abundance mindset). If this seems overly simplistic, that's because it is. An abundance mindset is always optimistic, no matter the circumstance.

I often tell Danielle, "We're just getting started." I sincerely mean it. Even when I'm eighty years old, I want to have the same mindset of "just getting started, just getting some momentum," because I believe my future will always be brighter than my past. I encourage you to think and believe the same.

To give more than you take requires that same perspective, that same abundance mindset. If you don't believe your future's brighter, what behavior follows? You won't give or sacrifice more. The reason is fear of scarcity— you won't have enough. Anne Frank is known to have said, "No one has ever become poor by giving."

> *Abundance leads to a road of opportunity, while scarcity leads to a dead end.*

Giving more versus giving less is much like the difference between a river and a reservoir. A river is always moving, providing life to all it touches. The river gives more than it takes and flows in abundance. But a reservoir doesn't move. It provides no life and ultimately kills anything that lives within it. The reservoir gives less than it takes and creates scarcity.

Be like a river—give more than you take, and abundance will follow. It was true for Mark Cole, and it's true for you. Wherever you are in life right now, wherever you are in your career journey, make a decision today. Whatever you're getting paid today, always give more than what's expected or required. Because when things get tough, guess what happens? The people who give more don't get fired or let go. Abundance leads to a road of opportunity, while scarcity leads to a dead end.

FOUR WAYS TO EXCHANGE

When it comes to the exchange of giving and taking, the experience of the receiver can vary greatly. How much of a difference does giving more have for those who stand to receive it? Let's explore the answer with a few scenarios. Imagine you visit four different types of car washes. At each car wash, you pay twenty dollars, leave the car keys, and are asked to return in twenty minutes.

Car Wash #1: When you return, you get back a dirty car. They didn't clean it at all—the crumbs are still on the inside and the outside is filthy. The car wash essentially stole your money.

This is *criminal exchange*: Car Wash #1 took but gave no value in return.

Car Wash #2: When you return, the car is mostly clean, but the tires and bottom of the exterior are still dirty. They gave you some value, but you're not happy.

This is *partial exchange*: Car Wash #2 took but gave partial value in return.

Car Wash #3: When you return, the car's clean on the inside and outside—it was vacuumed and washed thoroughly. You drive away satisfied.

This is *fair exchange*: Car Wash #3 took and gave fair value in return.

Car Wash #4: This time, before you leave, the attendant introduces himself and invites you to stay at their amenity-filled lounge while you wait. When you return, the car's clean on the inside and outside just like with Car Wash #3. But it gets better. The attendant hands you a $10 bill they found in your car. In addition, he informs you the car wash leveled out the air pressure in your tires and refilled the car's windshield washer fluid. Last, the attendant provides you a 25 percent off coupon for your next visit. You had an amazing experience and are likely to return for a second car wash.

This is *exchange in abundance*: Car Wash #4 took but gave far more value in return.

Now, think about this in your own life. Are you engaging in fair exchange, or are you exchanging in abundance? You might think giving fair value is honest, and you'd be right. But fair exchange has limitations. Just think about any time you've waited in a long line to check out at a store. There's only one cashier working, and you naturally wonder why without having any context for the situation.

Suddenly, another cashier opens an additional checkout line. This person is on his lunch break but decides to give more than he takes in pay. He instantly becomes every customer's hero. It would be a fair exchange not to open that additional checkout line. After all, the person is on break. Said differently, one checkout line is fair exchange. But the decision to open a second line is exchange in abundance. The second cashier gave more to waiting patrons.

> Fair exchange is appropriate, but to add greater value, choose to exchange in abundance.

Consider another scenario where you and I both have a dollar and we swap them back and forth—you give me your dollar, and I give you mine. We do this for a half hour and by the end, we're both frustrated. Why? Because we walked away tired and with the same amount of value. Fair exchange is nothing more than an equal game of "swap until you drop" in the long run. Would you want to engage with people or businesses that only provide you with equal value (and nothing more) in return? Fair exchange is appropriate, but to add greater value, choose to exchange in abundance.

When it comes to ways of exchange, giving more than you take is the game changer. Picture this: You're hired by a company for a salary of $100,000 per year. Multiply that number if you make more or divide it if you make less. Now, the company wants to see an exchange in abundance. They're not looking for fair value, like the "swap until you drop" scenario we described. This is what most people get wrong. The company gave you $100,000 and is expecting a $100,000-plus return on its investment. The *plus* is the difference between staying where you are and advancing nine positions, as Mark Cole did in our story earlier.

Is there a formula for *plus*? I'm a big believer in a 4:1 ratio, giving four times more than we take. Whether that's an employer with an employee, a company with a business, or a business with a customer, the 4:1 ratio applies. So, if they give us $100,000, we give back a minimum of $400,000 in value. This is what exchange in abundance looks like.

Let's connect this with our earlier lesson on purpose. Exchanging in abundance, particularly in a 4:1 ratio, becomes easy when we are driven by purpose. When purpose guides giving, abundance is a natural way of living.

Look no further than restaurant chain Chick-fil-A as an example. Its corporate purpose statement says it all: "To glorify God by being a faithful steward of all that is entrusted to us and to have a positive influence on all who come in contact with Chick-fil-A."[18]

Because the company wants to be a good steward to people, giving in abundance is second nature. It has a reputation of going above and beyond to serve its customers, community, and employees through superior customer service, philanthropic initiatives, and profit-sharing programs.

STEPS TO FOLLOW

It's easy to want to take more than we give. That's natural; everyone does that. But if we want to stand out and get ahead in our career and life, here are three practical steps to giving more than we take.

Step 1—Be the First to Give

Why do we have to wait to give? Just give. We'll find abundance and opportunity when we say yes to going first, to stepping out and giving first. And we may not always see the fruit of giving first. This is okay. If you planted a seed today, would you come back tomorrow to dig it up? Of course not. The problem is, people expect to plant today and reap tomorrow. That's not how things work in nature, and it's certainly not how they work in the world either. You plant today, nurture and water the seed tomorrow, and *eventually* the seed sprouts. The scarcity mindset plucks the seed now. But the abundance mindset is optimistic about the future harvest.

The people who are best at giving more than they take always give first. You can do the same. Plant the seed first. I encourage you to be the first to give more value, care, love, help, etc. Be first in acts of kindness, in helping someone, in showing support, in extending your

> *Whatever you're doing, just give more—and be the first to do it.*

hand, or in simply saying, "I love you." Whatever you're doing, just give more—and be the first to do it.

Step 2—Apply the 4:1 Ratio to All Relationships

Apply the 4:1 ratio with all your personal and professional relationships—including with your spouse, family members, friends, team members, employer, and clients. This could mean going the extra mile at work, offering compliments to others, or providing support to family members. Whatever the context, give four times more than you take.

Step 3—Pay Attention to What Matters to Others

We tend to underestimate just how different everyone is. Each person is built uniquely. Just look at your fingerprint compared to others'. If we're going to effectively give more to others, we have to pay attention to what matters most to them.

There are five common things that generally matter to people. Each is best described in the book *The 5 Languages of Appreciation in the Workplace* by Gary Chapman and Paul White.[19] The five languages reflect ways to express and receive appreciation in professional settings. Serving as a practical framework for identifying what matters most to others, they will serve us well in giving more than we take. Here they are, paraphrased in brief:

#1: Words of Affirmation

As a person of faith, I truly believe there is the power of life and death in our words. They can build people up and tear them down. If you recognize that words of affirmation matter to someone, this is how you can best give to that person: affirm them. Tell them, "Good job," "I appreciate you," "I admire your talents," or whatever the occasion calls for. They can't know what they're doing matters unless you tell them. Verbal or written expressions of appreciation such as praise, encouragement, gratitude, and recognition all matter. Our words of affirmation can come in many forms. Most importantly, however, is our authenticity in such words. We must take good care to mean and express them at the right times.

#2: Quality Time

Spending focused time with someone is also a show of appreciation. Consider whether quality time matters to someone. You may give them words of affirmation, but those words will fall short. With a "quality time" person, maybe all you need to do is say, "Do you want to join me for lunch today?" That will pique his or her attention because you've identified what matters most. Quality time doesn't have to be complicated. It can simply be having a conversation, going for a walk, or sharing a meal, so long as you're present and engaged in the time spent.

#3: Appropriate Physical Gestures

Appropriate physical gestures communicate support, comfort, reassurance, and value. In the workplace, it can include a pat on the back, high five, or handshake. With my team, I'll sometimes tap someone's shoulder and say, "Great job," or put my arm around another and say, "You're crushing it."

As a side note, knowing your own language of appreciation as well as that of the person you're working with helps change the game.

For example, many years ago Danielle would come to my office when I was very busy and bring me a cup of coffee and some fruit. Oftentimes, I would say, "No thank you." This would offend her. She thought I was being rude or unappreciative.

We both failed to realize our respective languages of appreciation. When I was busy or stressed, I was seeking a physical gesture of comfort, not an act of service like bringing me coffee.

Danielle was trying to add value, but it wasn't valuable to me. But when she started realizing physical gestures mattered most, she replaced the coffee and fruit with an encouraging pat on the back. When I'm in a stressful situation and we're working together, this energizes me.

#4: Acts of Service

Acts of service involve showing your appreciation by doing something you know the other person cares about. In the previous example, Danielle would bring me coffee and fruit; she's an "acts of service" person, demonstrating appreciation through helpful actions. This is not only what matters to her but also how she gives more. When I finally realized this, I found ways to serve her.

Why? To give more than I take, I aligned with what matters to her—one of the main reasons why I make the bed every morning. (Now when I don't make the bed, Danielle thinks I'm mad at her!) In all seriousness, if we are going to effectively give more than we take, we should seek to give what matters most to people.

#5: Giving Tangible Gifts
Giving tangible gifts is simply that—giving someone a physical gift of appreciation. The gift is meant to show that you were thinking of the other person. To a "tangible gifts" person, it indicates you value him or her. This may include a thankyou card, small present, or other physical token of appreciation. A friend on my team named Ray is a "tangible gifts" person. So, whenever I have the opportunity to give more to him, I keep this in mind. On one occasion, I found a nice pair of summer shoes and bought two pairs—one for him and one for me. The shoes weren't a huge gift and didn't cost a lot, but the gesture meant the world to him.

The reason I outline these steps, specifically the last one, is because we can't possibly add value to people if we don't know what they value. Therefore, sometimes giving more than you take is really about recognizing what matters to people. The simplest way to figure this out is to ask. And if you don't want to ask, just observe people. About 80 to 90 percent of people do what *they* find valuable. For example, if the person gives gifts, they're likely a "tangible gifts" person. Or if the person wants to spend time together, they're a "quality time" person. Does the person always want to shake hands? You guessed it— they're an "appropriate physical gestures" person. And if he or she wants to do something for you to make life easier? They're probably an "acts of service" person.

People don't always recognize what matters to others. As a result, they use the wrong language to show appreciation. You don't want to share words of affirmation when it's quality time that they value, or vice versa. But when you get it right, it's like magic.

I've experienced this firsthand. For so many years, I was holding back the potential of our organization because I didn't understand this concept. I gave to people what I thought was valuable without taking the time to identify what mattered to them. As a result, my giving only resonated with a small percentage of the population. However, every effort today is made to identify what is valuable to people—clients and employees alike. The result has been nothing short of amazing.

Remember my earlier story on the 500 percent increase in revenue? This can be just the start in your life. I encourage you to pay attention to what matters to people, be the first to give, and do it in a 4:1 ratio whenever possible. Everything starts to get better from there.

GO FORTH HUMBLY & GIVE ABUNDANTLY

It has been said before, and you will hear it again: it is better to give than to receive.[20] But to give more than we take, we must first have an abundance mindset. When we operate from a place of abundance, there's always more to go around. When we have an abundance mindset, we can move to giving in abundance. And if we are willing to take the right steps, we can effectively give to people what matters most. Take the time to learn what's valuable and assume nothing.

There's a saying that's often attributed to Winston Churchill: "We make a living by what we get, but we make a life by what we give." With this in mind, I encourage you to go forth humbly and give abundantly. Give with an open heart and watch as your life and the lives of those around you grow in abundance.

5

Great Commitments Precede Great Achievements

There is a simple truth at the heart of any success: achievement never comes without great commitment. Without a deep commitment to and steadfast determination toward a goal, it's unlikely we can achieve the kind of greatness we're destined for. Commitments are powerful influences over our decisions, day in and day out. Those decisions, in turn, can move us closer to our grand vision regardless of circumstance.

TRUE DETERMINATION

There is a story about a Georgia boy born into poverty in 1921 who would one day come to represent the true power of commitment *and* achievement. This boy's commitment from an early age was to serve people, beginning with his family. His career started in the kitchen of a boarding house he helped his mother run. By 1929, at the age of eight, he started a business of selling Coca-Cola bottles to people in his neighborhood. At the age of twelve, he had a newspaper route to support his family. Think about that—a twelve-year-old supporting his family. By fourteen, he and his brothers became the primary breadwinners for the family. At eighteen, he was drafted into the US Army and remained there until 1945, when he was twenty-four. The next year, he and his brothers pooled their resources—$4,200 plus a $6,400 loan from a local bank—to open a local restaurant on May 23, 1946. Three years later, his two brothers were killed in a tragic plane accident. In 1959, at the age of thirty-eight, married and the father of three, he was diagnosed with colon cancer. One year later, his restaurant burned to the ground.

This is the story of Chick-fil-A founder Truett Cathy.

Through all the years and change, Truett Cathy's commitment remained serving people. In fact, Cathy often said he wasn't in the *chicken* business; he was in the *people* business. Fast forward to 2022, and Chick-fil-A (famous for its chicken sandwiches) is consistently one of the most profitable and successful fast-food franchises with more than two thousand locations and award-winning customer service.[21]

Each US Chick-fil-A store on average is also more profitable than your average Starbucks, McDonald's, and Subway combined.[22] What's more, Chick-fil-A accomplishes this with one less day of operation per week versus its competitors because of the company's commitment to staying closed on Sundays.

How does the company do it? Through great commitments, which include an overarching desire to have a positive impact on customers and communities alike. Cathy would regularly say, "You can do anything if you want to bad enough." The result is one of the most successful quick-service restaurant chains ever, a remarkable achievement considering Truett Cathy's humble beginnings.

The Chick-fil-A story is often told in leadership and business books. Why use it here? Because it intersects with many of the important lessons we've discussed so far. Chick-fil-A chose to be intentionally good in building a people-centric business model. That model was predicated on valuing people first in order to add value to them. The journey wasn't smooth—Truett Cathy had his fair share of problems. However, he decided to make his purpose, what he believed was a calling to serve, bigger. In fact, one of Chick-fil-A's company philosophies embodies giving more than you take. It's called a "Giving Philosophy," and it does not expect anything in return.[23] The culmination of these lessons reinforced great commitments. It's no wonder Chick-fil-A has been able to achieve great success.

COMMITMENT IS POWERFUL

Consider this staggering statistic backed by research from the University of Scranton. Only 8 percent of people who create New Year's resolutions actually achieve them.[24] The majority, specifically 92 percent, fall short. Do you wonder what that 8 percent did differently? After all, everyone who creates a resolution starts out motivated. The answer is most likely found in one powerful word: *commitment*. As Jim Rohn often says, "Motivation is what gets you started. Commitment is what keeps you going."

Let's take the example of going to the gym. Every January, many people make resolutions to start exercising. But *resolutions* are merely quality decisions to either do or not do something. *Commitments*, on the other hand, are acts of dedication. This is the difference: out of every hundred people at the gym who start out motivated, ninety-two of them are likely only *resolving* while the other eight are also *committing*. Think about that for a moment. Everyone made a resolution or decision. But only eight people took the next step to turn it into a commitment—a complete game changer.

> Motivation is what gets you started. Commitment is what keeps you going.

Great commitments are powerful. They make the difference between success or failure at work, in school, and with your family at home. What happens when we fall short of our commitments? Not only does our self-worth suffer, but others may also lose trust in us. And for the 92 percent who fall short in our statistic above, on average they are more likely to make excuses, blame others, and be easily distracted. But when we are greatly committed to and then achieve something, there is a tremendous feeling of fulfillment that follows. With each success come positive shifts, from how we feel about ourselves to our relationships with others.

A FORMULA FOR ACHIEVEMENT

What if I told you there is a formula for great achievements? It's not complicated. In fact, it's one of the simplest formulas you'll ever need to know, because it includes concepts you're likely familiar with. Here it is:

Vision + Choices + Detailed Plan +
Accountability = Great Achievements

Great commitments precede great achievements, right? Then vision, choices, a detailed plan, and accountability are the great commitments required of you. Each precedes great achievements in our formula.

Throughout the rest of the chapter, let's break each part of this achievement formula down to get a better understanding of how each aspect contributes to our success.

VISION

***Vision** + Choices + Detailed Plan +*
Accountability = Great Achievements

Let's familiarize ourselves with vision in greater detail. There are five key points to cover.

#1–Vision Helps Us Focus on the Bigger Picture

As I mentioned previously, people often overestimate what can be accomplished in a day and underestimate what can be achieved in a career or lifetime. The long-term view is always discounted. That said, success is not a one-day story. Great achievements tend to occur over long periods of time. To bridge the gap between commitment and time, we need vision. It is vision that helps us stay focused on the big picture.

Danielle and I adopted a vision years ago to help us maintain the big picture. We have set a three-hundred-year vision for ourselves. Now, I don't mean that to sound unrealistic. It's simply the idea that our purpose outlives us. In other words, we are looking to do things that have an impact beyond our lifetime. The vision is broken down into phases based on age, spanning decades and years.

- Phase 1: birth to 21
- Phase 2: 22 to 39

- Phase 3: 40 to 49
- Phase 4: 50 to 59
- Phase 5: 60 to 69
- Phase 6: 70 to 100
- Phase 7: 101 to 200
- Phase 8: 201 to 300

Phase 7 is beyond our lifetime, where we envision achievement: our organizations and the leaders we've developed make the world better than we left it. Everything preceding this point reflects commitments. In phase 8, our mission of impacting the world continues to be carried out through our organizations, foundations, and future leaders.

I share this with you to illustrate a point. Visions, however big, can be broken down into parts. I start with decades and years. However, I also go to months and weeks, all the way down to hours. From there, I try to manage the minutes. By doing so, I make progress daily while staying focused on the long-term. Because if I can manage my minutes well, then my hours are going to go well. If my hours go well, then my day is going to go well, and so on. Days add up to years. Whether it's thirty days or three hundred years, the minutes matter.

I encourage you to also look at your life through a vision of your own creation. You don't need to have a three-hundred-year vision, but have a vision and break it down into phases—the more manageable you break it down, the easier it becomes.

#2–Vision Increases Consistency

If vision is the bridge between today and future achievement, consistency helps us cross it. Consistency holds us accountable, builds character, and tells people we can be trusted. Think about it. Anyone who's consistent is also thought to be trustworthy. And if we're trustworthy, achievement comes faster because people will help or follow someone they can trust.

The stronger the vision, the greater our consistency. That's because clarity helps us stay focused. We are more likely to stay true to our commitments and less likely

> *Vision is the bridge between today and future achievement; consistency helps us cross it.*

to be swayed or distracted by setbacks. So have a vision, clarify it, and consistency will follow.

#3–Vision Requires Patience

No farmer plants a seed today and expects a harvest tomorrow. That's because harvesting is a process preceded by commitment—namely toiling, planting, and nurturing.

You don't just plant and harvest; there's a preceding season of process. The same applies to vision. On the other side of vision is achievement, which in turn is preceded by a season of great commitment. Remember my three-hundred-year vision? There's one hundred years of commitment preceding achievement. Whatever your vision is, it requires a degree of patience to accomplish.

#4—Vision Dictates Priorities

This one is a close relative of point 2. In my life, the three-hundred-year vision for Danielle and me dictates our priorities. It shapes what we're willing to do and not do.

Without a clear vision of where we want to go or the direction in which we want to move, priorities can become very scattered. That's why we need to continually ask ourselves, *Am I moving closer to or farther away from my vision?* It keeps us honest and allows for adjustments. If our priorities don't align,

> With clear vision come crystal-clear priorities.

we need to get clearer on the vision. With clear vision come crystal-clear priorities. This is what makes vision a game changer on so many levels.

#5—Vision Increases Your Faith

Evangelist Myles Munroe sums up our last point well: "I think that the greatest gift God ever gave man is not the gift of sight but the gift of vision. Sight is a function of the eyes, but vision is a function of the heart."[25] While sight is a physical function, vision is something that comes from within. It allows us to see beyond the present moment and into the future. The clearer and more compelling that vision is, the more excited we are to achieve it.

> When your vision is written in your heart, your faith increases to achieve it.

In essence, vision is a foundation for progress. People who have great vision inherently accomplish more. Even if you don't know how you will do it, strive to have a great vision for what you want to achieve. Sight is as far as the eyes will allow, but vision is as far as the heart can see. When your vision is written in your heart, your faith increases to achieve it.

CHOICES

*Vision + **Choices** + Detailed Plan + Accountability = Great Achievements*

Life is a product of choices that compound one another. I made poor choices in the early part of my life and dealt with their consequences for many years. Poor choices lead to poor results, period. But when you make good choices consistently, you have more potential for greater results. And it doesn't even take great choices, just good ones—one after another.

Researchers Dr. Barbara Sahakian and Dr. Jamie Nicole LaBuzetta found:

- A child makes three thousand choices every day.
- In contrast, an adult makes thirty-five thousand choices every day.[26]

We are faced with so many different choices each day. Consider the number of responses to the following:

- who to spend time with, date, marry, vote for
- what to purchase, believe, eat, say
- when to commute, sleep, exercise, run errands
- where to travel, live, attend school, work

The list could go on and on. We are unaware of how many choices we make daily. Additional research from Cornell University's Dr. Brian Wansink and Dr. Jeffery Sobal estimates the average male makes a whopping 200 (at least) daily choices about food alone.[27] Personally, I give myself about 750 choices on food each day—something I should probably work on. If we're making 35,000 total choices, how many are good versus bad? As you can see, choices are a critical part of our formula.

Zig Ziglar reportedly said it best: "Your life is a result of the choices you have made. If you don't like your life, start making better choices." Don't beat yourself up for poor choices in the past. Just as I have since borne the fruit of good decisions, so can you. Each good decision you make going forward will build momentum toward great achievements.

DETAILED PLAN

*Vision + Choices + **Detailed Plan** +*
Accountability = Great Achievements

There is a great system I use for creating a detailed plan, outlined by an acronym I learned from John Maxwell and detailed in his book *The 21 Irrefutable Laws of Leadership*. It is called PLAN AHEAD:[28]

- *Predetermine what a win looks like*: In sports, we always know what a win is—it's what individuals and teams work toward in every scrimmage, game, or match. Otherwise, playing sports without keeping score is uninspiring. Life is no different. By not defining what a win looks like, you fall into the trap of being vague and avoiding accountability. If you want great achievements, define what those are up front.

- *Lay out your goals*: Once you know what a win looks like, set specific, measurable, realistic, and time-bound goals aligning to the achievement.
- *Adjust priorities*: Be prepared to be flexible. Focus on the most important tasks that will move you closer to your goals, but be willing to adapt in order to move ahead.
- *Notify key personnel*: Notify important people such as those on your team and in your family. Let them know what you're doing. This way, they will understand if you need to spend less time with them during this season of working toward your specific goal. Notifying them also keeps you accountable.
- *Allow time for acceptance*: If you move forward without allowing time for acceptance, you lose buy-in, and buy-in is the key for success as a leader.
- *Head into action*: This is the part that most people do well. They put a list together of what needs to get done and follow through on it.
- *Expect problems*: Setbacks are going to happen along the way. You need to expect that. Don't be surprised when problems occur. Instead, understand what may go wrong so you are not deflated if it occurs.
- *Always point to successes*: Celebrate the wins along the way, no matter how big or small. Pointing to

your successes is an act of acknowledgment that you are on the right track. This helps keep you and those around you energized and focused.

- *Daily review progress*: Make it a habit to assess progress toward goals on a daily basis. This helps you determine if you're on track, allowing for adjustments if needed.

I encourage you to create a detailed plan, leveraging the PLAN AHEAD acronym. To do so is to have a strategy that is actionable, increasing the chances of any great achievement.

ACCOUNTABILITY

Vision + Choices + Detailed Plan +
Accountability = Great Achievements

Let's recap our formula up to this point. With a clear vision, good choices, and comprehensive plan, we set ourselves up for success. But accountability has the power to turn the vision we start with into reality. Consider the following research findings from the Association for Talent Development on the success rate of achieving a goal and the role of accountability:

- Having an idea or goal: 10%
- Consciously deciding that you will do it: 25%
- Deciding when you will do it: 40%

- Planning how to do it: 50%
- Committing to someone that you will do it: 65%[29]

Accountability is key—most people never commit to someone else to hold them accountable. As a result, they only succeed on average between 10 and 50 percent of the time. But by committing to someone, you succeed an average 65 percent of the time. Now, there's one more statistic from this same study I want you to consider: to reach a success rate of 95 percent, one must make an "accountability appointment" with the person to whom they are committed.[30] Said differently, by having a scheduled accountability appointment with someone, you only have a 5 percent chance of not reaching your goal. So, the aim is not only telling the person (65 percent rate of success)

> *Have a scheduled "accountability appointment" for a 95 percent chance of succeeding.*

but also meeting with him or her regularly (95 percent rate of success). Knowing this, would you now commit to an accountability appointment with someone?

Continually increase your probability of winning by holding yourself accountable. Don't just have a goal or idea; get specific. Decide on what, when, and how (detailed plan). Then, find an accountability partner and commit to them that you're going to do it. Say, "Every week, on this day and time, let's meet—and please hold me accountable." But don't just say it. Meet with them regularly until you succeed.

GREAT ACHIEVEMENTS

Vision + Choices + Detailed Plan +
Accountability = **Great Achievements**

Great achievements are not accomplished by great activities or hard work alone. I know a lot of people who work really hard but don't accomplish much. Succeeding starts with being awakened, empowered, and equipped with the tools to reach your potential. And potential? That's your area of giftedness that we've discussed at length. This is where we want to operate from. After all, we can only hope for mediocrity in an area of weakness.

Great commitments, when aligned to your giftedness, maximize your potential for achievement. From there, you pair them with vision, choices, a detailed plan, and a process for accountability—our formula. The end result doesn't have to be something amazing or big. Reaching your potential is the ultimate success.

Returning to an example I referenced earlier, potential is like a gas tank: whether you have a car with a ten-gallon tank or a 737 jetliner with a capacity of four thousand gallons, all that matters is that you maximize it, because we are each designed for different purposes.

So, what size gas tank do you have?

Many years ago, Myles Munroe shared a powerful message on potential, starting with a question that changed my life: Where is the wealthiest part of the world? The answer, according to him, is the cemetery. He explained: "There lie buried companies

Reaching your potential is the ultimate success.

that were never started, inventions that were never made, bestselling books that were never written, and masterpieces that were never painted. In the cemetery is buried the greatest treasure of untapped potential."[31]

I want to encourage you to rob the cemetery by fulfilling your potential. I don't want you to try to be a four-thousand-gallon gas tank if you only have the capacity of fifty gallons. But I also don't want you to compare yourself to a person who has a ten-gallon gas tank. If you have a fifty-gallon gas tank, use it all. Become who you were designed to be. Make great commitments on the front end to create great achievements on the back end.

THE NEXT STEPS

Let's now outline the steps to follow based on what we've covered thus far.

Step 1—(Vision) Create a Vision Board for Your Life

Danielle and I created a vision board fifteen years ago, and I still carry it in my binder today. I look at it each time I complete my Daily Game Planner that I discussed in chapter 1. This is a daily habit that has immense value in helping me be intentionally good.

There is great value in having a vision board. We are, in turn, able to narrow decisions and priorities to what's most important: the dreams for what we want to create in life.

I believe all of us had great dreams as children. But people tend to stop dreaming over time. If you have stopped, I ask that you start again—have dreams that will allow you to fulfill your potential. You can start with a vision board of pictures and words that serve as motivators and reminders. It is a visual technique that has served me well in putting action behind my dreams, and I'm confident it will do the same for you.

Step 2—(Choices) Choose Every Day to Make Better Decisions in All Areas of Your Life

Making better decisions starts with how we spend our time. What are we reading or listening to? Who are we spending the most time with? Is the sum of our time adding up to creating a better life?

I encourage you to be very selective with your time. For example, consider the people you spend time with. The five closest people to you will wind up being your future, shaping your beliefs, attitudes, and habits. So be selective in who you spend time with and where you spend your time as well. For example, do you spend time on your strengths or on your weaknesses? Remember, in your area of weakness, you will likely start at poor and the best you'll get is average. But in your area of giftedness, you start at average with the ability to become excellent.

As a person of faith, I spend time daily with God and the Bible. It helps me gain clarity, direction, and purpose for the day. This makes all the difference for me. If I don't do this, I can't fulfill the vision God has given me.

Step 3—(Detailed Plan) See Everyone as a "10"

Consider any major achievement you want to reach in your lifetime. It's going to take people. We simply can't accomplish anything of great significance without them. Just look at history—anything of significance throughout time, on average, has been accomplished through collaboration. So, in returning to our earlier lesson of valuing people to add value to them, start with seeing everyone as a "10."

Next, choose one major achievement that you want to accomplish. The time frame for it can be flexible—one year, five years, thirty years, or three hundred years from now. Choose one major achievement and create a detailed plan using Maxwell's PLAN AHEAD system. In fact, look in your calendar right now and reserve time for when you're going to create that achievement. Identify that one thing, and then build out the plan. And remember, no great achievement is accomplished alone.

Step 4—(Accountability) Choose Your Accountability Partner

I have accountability partners in different areas of my life. For example, Danielle and I are accountability partners to each other in the area of finances. She has access to every account I have and vice versa. She has full transparency to all transactions because we share usernames and passwords. She can check each account at any time to see my spending activity, and I can do the same.

This ensures we are not working against each other. If Danielle ends up saving money on something, she can feel confident I'm not going to offset it with any surprise expense. I know married couples where one spouse doesn't know about accounts that the other has. I compare this to driving a car with one eye closed—it might work for a while, but eventually you could crash.

Danielle and I are accountability partners in business as well. Through our leadership coaching company, Lions

Pride Leadership, we also keep business owners and business leaders alike accountable in the area of leadership. And for leaders, accountability is especially important—to our team members, clients, customers, managers, and any other stakeholders.

I have an accountability partner in the area of health. The partner, also someone I mentor, holds me accountable for exercise and diet. This is an area I struggle with. Remember those 750 choices I give myself each day? Honestly, I'm a "foodie"—I love food. But I acknowledge I need to make better choices if I want to see my three-hundred-year vision through to at least the first one hundred years.

Finally, I have multiple accountability partners in the area of faith. There are three people who consistently check in on me and say, "How are you doing in these areas of life when it comes to your walk with God?" or "How are you applying your faith in marriage?" They are instrumental in my journey to grow into the person God designed me to be.

Accountability partners changed my life, and they have the ability to do the same for you. I have found the greatest benefit by having ones in the areas of finances, business, leadership, health, and faith. But there's no shortage of things you can choose to focus on. I encourage you to establish your own accountability partners today.

Step 5—(Great Achievement) Better Understand Your Giftedness

You'll never accomplish what you should in your areas of weakness. Great achievements happen only in areas of strength and giftedness. If you recall, giftedness is three things: mission, competency, and style. Mission is what you're passionate about (your what). Competency is what you're good at (your why). Style is how you and others perceive you (your how).

My friend Mike recently shared a story about himself and his wife. His wife asked him to put together a piece of furniture. His response was, "I can't do that because it's outside my area of giftedness."

Now, he was joking—at least a little. But he has recognized and embraced operating in his area of strength. What he was really saying to his wife was, "I want to focus on what I'm good at."

Is there something to be said about improving in areas we are not good at? Sure. But focusing on our strengths will bring in more resources to hire others who can perform what we are not good at. In turn, we actually bless others as well. We empower them to operate in their giftedness, a win-win for everyone. This is true abundance.

You may have heard the quote, "Everybody is a genius. But if you judge a fish by its ability to climb a tree, it will live its whole life believing that it is stupid." Many of us today are doing the same—climbing when we should be swimming. The simple truth is, we are not designed to succeed in an area of weakness—we're destined to excel in our giftedness. This is how we bring value to the world. I encourage you to recognize and move forward in your unique giftedness. Doing so will open your life to new and abundant opportunities that align with your strengths.

START WALKING

Returning to where we started, Truett Cathy, the founder of Chick-fil-A, was really good at investing in people. Cathy devised a model of developing team members to become all they were designed to be. This required great commitment, but it resulted in extraordinary achievement. As you are on this journey to accomplish great achievement, recognize your gift, and then put in the hours to develop it. We outlined the steps. Let's now start walking.

Years ago, I had vision and wishful thinking. I did not realize the great commitment that vision (God's plan) required. But with commitment, everything became clearer. I now realize that great achievements require great sacrifice. I encourage you today to do the same. Make a great commitment on the front end—put your head down and do the work. You can make no greater investment.

With great commitments, you will be witness to great achievements in your lifetime. And as you see your vision come to fruition, I encourage you to pay it forward by helping others in their own journey toward achieving their dreams.

A word from the author

Role vs Identity

What you do is not who you are. Imagine a great, tall oak tree with sprawling branches that kiss the sky. See it from the very top all the way down to the bottom and its roots. Now, imagine at the base of the tree, there's a fish—let's say it's a blue marlin, one of the largest and most beautiful aquatic animals. The marlin is struggling to climb the tree, flapping its fins frantically. And as time passes, the fish grows more frustrated and unhappy because nothing seems to be working out. Despite its splendor, the marlin is destined to fail. Why? Because fish were never meant to climb trees. They were born to glide gracefully in water. No matter how much that marlin tries, it will never succeed in climbing a tree the way a squirrel would.

THE TRUE YOU

Have you ever felt like the marlin who hopelessly flopped along? When we talk about role versus identity, it's so important not to confuse whatever role we are playing in life at a moment in time for our identity. Role and identity in the instance of the mar-lin, for example, are completely distinct. This likewise applies to you and me. Sure, your role can play a big part

> *Who you are goes far beyond what you do.*

in your life, but it's not who you are. Who you are goes far beyond what you do. Understanding this is the first step in separating role versus identity.

Consider the following insights from a *Harvard Business Review* study on self-awareness. In a series of ten investigations with nearly five thousand participants, the research revealed some surprising insights. Despite the fact that most people *believe* they are self-aware, the study found that only 10 to 15 percent of those studied actually fit the criteria for self-awareness.[32] This underscores how difficult it may be for us to separate our role in life from our identity.

The more self-aware we are, the more ability we have to recognize what's happening around us. So, when it comes to the concept of role versus identity, it's important to understand that our identity is made up of our self-concept, which includes our self-worth and ego. It's our beliefs, values, and traits that make us who we are at the core. That is not the same as the roles we play, whether it's a spouse, parent, business leader, and so on.

Most people tend to connect their role to their identity. This is role-based identity, and it can be an issue. For example, if we are failing in a role, we associate that shortcoming with self-worth. When this happens, we unintentionally surrender power and influence over our lives to external factors and other people. But any failure experienced in a role does not define who we are by design. Knowing this allows for you to instead run the day.

THE PITFALLS OF ROLE-BASED IDENTITY

The danger of equating our role with our identity cannot be overstated. Following are some of the reasons to separate the two. It serves us well to pay close attention here. Otherwise, the self-imposed limitations that result will hinder our potential, personal growth, and ultimate fulfillment in life.

The Performance Trap

The first reason to separate role and identity is to avoid the *performance trap*. That's the vicious cycle where you're trying and getting frustrated, just like our blue marlin. Nothing seems to work. This can lead to self-deprecating thoughts such as, *I'll never amount to much*, or, *I'm a failure*. Negative voices tend to keep yapping away. We try to solve the problem through performance. This is a trap we can rise above by separating role from identity.

My identity is not wrapped up in my role. Furthermore, any associated motivation for performing well is not tied to a desire to influence how others see me. The Bible says I am made in God's image.[33] So, not diminishing my identity gives glory to Him. In other words, our worth is God-given, not role-determined or performance-driven. You don't have to share my beliefs, but please know this: identity and role have to be separate.

> *Our worth is God-given, not role-determined or performance-driven.*

The Battle for Our Attention

The second reason for separating role and identity is the ever-growing and seemingly perpetual competition for our minds. Consider the world in which we live today with marketers seeking to capture our attention (and dollars). Companies such as Meta or TikTok, like many other online media platforms, operate to some degree as marketers. The longer they can keep you on their platforms, the greater their likelihood of not only harvesting your personal data but also monetizing that data via targeted ads that result in a transaction. None of this necessarily makes these companies bad; it's simply part of an operating model.

Now, just think how much easier it is to move people toward a desired action when identity and role are blurred. If those seeking our attention can successfully wrap a role in identity, then emotional actions (namely online purchases) are more easily thought of as rational decisions rather than impulsive choices.

Conditioned to Seek Approval

People are far too often becoming conditioned to care too much about the approval of others. In a world where social media rules, "views," "likes," and/or "followers" have become incredibly important. Just think about any time you have ever posted something online. Did you check to see the number of likes or views you received? If people don't get enough of any combination, they may not feel as valuable as those who receive more. We can become captive to this approval-seeking system.

If you have ever struggled with this, I encourage you to go deeper to better understand why this may be important to you. Consider breaking free from this system. Doing so can be the difference between falling short and propelling yourself forward in life.

What Society Says

The last reason to distinguish your role from your identity is what society says, which is that how we perform our roles should dictate how we feel about and see ourselves. I don't conform to that belief whatsoever.

We need to view *ourselves* as a "10," just as we view others. All the time. My identity does not get affected by my performance. However, my role could fluctuate up and down. Sometimes I'm performing well as a business owner, and sometimes I'm not. Sometimes I'm performing well as a husband, and sometimes I'm not. We all have highs and lows in our respective roles. But I throw caution to then transferring that to how we feel about ourselves. Your identity should be as sturdy as an anchor that holds a ship steady. Keep it at a perfect "10" to sail confidently or the waves will sink it to a mere "1."

THE 4 TYPES OF "ROLE" PEOPLE

Keeping roles separate from identity is important. That said, we can further enhance our livelihood by consciously choosing how we approach our roles. To simplify this choice, there are four key types of roles to consider: Dividers, Subtracters, Adders, and Multipliers.[34]

Role 1: Dividers (100 ÷ 10 = 10)

Imagine you give someone 100 units of something and they turn it into 10 through division. We call this a Divider.

The Divider has separated something into parts. Nothing greater has been created. If anything, what they started with has become diluted. In practice, Dividers create division and oftentimes conflict. Examples include playing favorites, pitting people against each other, or refusing to listen to different viewpoints. Ultimately, Dividers are left with far less than they started with.

Role 2: Subtracters (100 – 10 = 90)

Subtracters are a close relative of Dividers. They take one number away from the other. Both Dividers and Subtracters operate with a scarcity mindset.

Subtracters remove value, creating more problems than they solve and adding nothing. Examples include negativity and an overall lack of effort and appreciation for people and events. While their impact is not as damaging as Dividers, Subtracters pull down the morale of all in their path.

Role 3: Adders (100 + 10 = 110)

Adders add something to something else. Adders align to abundance. They add value, making things better and improving outcomes—the opposite of Subtracters. Examples include going above and beyond with energy and enthusiasm. Adders contribute to the overall ecosystem.

Role 4: Multipliers (100 x 10 = 1,000)

Multipliers add tremendous exponential growth. They can start with the same 100 units and convert them into 1,000. Big difference.

Multipliers amplify value. They create synergy and enhance everyone around them, leading to extraordinary results—the polar opposite of Dividers. Examples include inspiring and empowering others to achieve more than they originally thought possible. The Multiplier's influence is essentially multiplied many times over by those whose paths they cross.

We can divide and falter, subtract and suppress, add and grow, or multiply in abundance. Ultimately, the choice is clear: choose to be a Multiplier in everything you do. Lift others up, and you'll soon see farther standing on their shoulders than you can alone.

BUILDING A HEALTHY IDENTITY

Let's shift our focus now to identity, the other side of the coin. Building a healthy identity is truly important in the realm of our overall well-being and capacity to live a fulfilling life. Let's review five key areas, which are referenced in Multi-Health Systems Inc.'s emotional intelligence assessment called EQ-i 2.0 (Emotional Quotient-Inventory 2.0): self-perception, self-expression, interpersonal skills, decision-making, and stress management.[35]

Area #1: Self-Perception

Self-perception starts with respecting ourselves and includes attitudes, beliefs, and feelings about ourselves. When self-regard is high, we are more confident. People who are more confident perform better. Naturally, the opposite also holds true. That's why as leaders, we have a responsibility to do everything possible to ensure our people's self-perception is healthy. This underscores the importance of separating identity from role.

Of equal importance is the pursuit of meaning and self-improvement, which contributes to a healthy self-perception. When we are lifelong learners and develop ourselves daily, we attain a greater sense of our true identity.

Last, self-perception requires developing emotional self-awareness and a better understanding of our own emotions. Consider low emotional intelligence. It is typically associated with low self-perception. When emotions are high, the reality of a situation may become distorted. It's just like a roller coaster, with highs and lows. We can easily get carried away. Therefore, high emotional self-awareness is key to building up our identity. By recognizing and managing our emotions well, we protect our identity and become more effective leaders.

> *By recognizing and managing our emotions well, we protect our identity and become more effective leaders.*

Area #2: Self-Expression

Effective self-expression is vital to leading well. Have you ever been around someone who couldn't communicate what he or she was thinking? And, as a result, you felt their frustration? When we lack the ability to effectively express ourselves, our identity can be affected.

A person who can communicate their feelings, beliefs, and thoughts in an effective manner has a higher probability of success in life. The better we communicate, the better relationships we have with people. And the better our relationships, the better we feel about ourselves. I believe each one of us is designed to have positive relationships with others.

Area #3: Interpersonal Skills

Strong interpersonal skills translate to better relationships. When we have better relationships, we feel better overall. When we feel better, we act better—it's a beautiful cycle. An important aspect here is empathy, which relates to our understanding and appreciation for how others feel. Showing a high degree of empathy lets others know we value them.

Area #4: Decision-Making

Our ability to solve problems or find solutions is optimized when emotions are less prone to hijack our decisions. When we are able to clearly recognize the distinct difference between our role and identity, we make better decisions.

The ability to see things objectively can also be affected if we don't make the effort to separate role and identity. I know this firsthand because I struggled to separate the two. As a result, I made many poor decisions early in my life. But when I finally recognized this, everything changed.

Identity is a constant—it's who God says we are. And with an ability to see things objectively, we are more likely to be effective in our roles.

Last, resisting the temptation to act on our emotions—whether that means delaying purchases, controlling the desire to shout, or avoiding drugs or alcohol—contributes to an overall increased sense of self-worth. When done well, we come to embrace who we truly are.

Area #5: Stress Management

The ability to handle stress is key to rounding out a healthy identity. There are three parts to this: flexibility, stress tolerance, and optimism.

Flexibility is the ability to adapt our emotions, thoughts, and behaviors. When we are confident in our identity, we will navigate life differently. We are individually more adaptable to whatever external stimulus may come.

In the same respect, stress tolerance—our ability to cope with stressful situations—is higher. When you can deal with stress, it will change your life for the better.

Optimism, a positive attitude and outlook, comes from positive self-identity. You simply don't find people with both an optimistic outlook and a negative identity.

If we are to truly continue to grow and develop every day, it will serve us well to separate role from identity. If we don't, it can wreak havoc in our lives. Consider what happens when we have setbacks in our roles and those same roles are not separated from identity. Self-perception suffers, from confidence and ambition to the regulation of our emotional state.

In building up a healthy identity, we'll also want to improve in the areas of self-expression and interpersonal skills. Each contributes to how we see ourselves.

Also, there is a correlated benefit to decision-making and stress management when we build a healthy

Recognizing who you truly are is the key that unlocks your God-given potential.

sense of identity. I encourage you to focus on these areas of life and see your entire outlook change—because recognizing who you truly are is the key that unlocks your God-given potential.

BENEFITS OF A HEALTHY IDENTITY

There are many benefits to a healthy identity, which I'll now unpack. To be described in any of the following ways truly reflects knowing oneself. And in knowing oneself, it's not just us who gain in how we show up each day. A healthy identity blesses those around us by inspiring authenticity.

Fulfilled

In the words of the great philosopher Socrates, "To know thyself is the beginning of wisdom." Knowing ourselves empowers us to give our best every day. That's because self-knowledge is recognition of our own capabilities. In turn, we can maximize those capabilities.

Think about giftedness for a moment—when we lack a sense of identity, it's unlikely we're operating within our giftedness. We are not starting at good, with the ability to move to great. But when we not only know but also operate in our area of strength, life can be more fulfilling. We bring greater value to the world.

Truthful

When we have a healthy identity, authenticity comes naturally. Consider dishonesty. It is a self-defense mechanism to protect or maintain something that is false. Dishonesty no longer applies when we know who we are. There's no false facade to maintain. Truth becomes a guiding light, enabling us and those we empower to stand firm and secure.

Happy

People with healthy identities tend to be happier. This is because they on average pursue things that matter to them. When we know ourselves, we can more aptly align our actions and interests to activities that lead to greater well-being and happiness—and happiness is contagious.

Have you ever noticed someone who had a *presence* about them? My wife exemplifies this, lifting the mood of a room with a flash of a smile, an infectious laugh, or words of optimism. Happiness has a way of radiating outward and affecting those around us.

Peaceful

I don't know about you, but feeling happy contributes to my inner peace. It should come as no surprise that happiness and peace are related to and reinforce each other. Both reflect a sense of contentment and well-being.

Happiness and peace may be experienced differently, but they can each arise from a similar source—a healthy identity. When our identities are strong, we are less likely to be swayed by external pressures or people. This can be a great source of tranquility and joy. In much the same way as happiness, peacefulness can be a source of strength and comfort to others. It has the power to defuse conflicts, promote harmony, and generate love.

Self-Controlled

Momentum is the *great exaggerator* because when we have it, we look better than we are and vice versa. The great thing about knowing who we are is this: we are always in control; we are self-controlled, regardless of momentum's forces.

Momentum does not inflate or deflate our perception of reality because of our strong sense of identity. And with that comes great discipline in being true to ourselves and others—in our finances, relationships, and faith, as well as in the traditions we make and keep. Just think of any situation where you can be an example to others. A lack of self-control can exacerbate problems and cause harm. Conversely, self-control can bring calmness to any situation. When we are self-controlled, we are a model of strength for others.

Friendly

When we know ourselves and are comfortable in our own skin, we become more friendly and approachable. This is not to say someone who is unfriendly has an unhealthy identity. People certainly have bad days. But I'm willing to bet anyone who is consistently unfriendly has a poor sense of identity. I'm likewise willing to say the opposite for someone who is friendly. Don't we love being around these people? Being friendly is a blessing to others. It allows them to feel seen and valued.

Caring

Caring is a reflection of values and priorities rooted in our unique identities. When identity is healthy, our capacity to be kind and compassionate to others is greater. More so, caring for others typically reinforces our own self-worth, regardless of whether the other person welcomes or receives the blessing.

Loyal

When we know who we are and what we believe in, we are willing to make great commitments to people or purposes. This can include loyalty to ourselves (for example, what we identify with, what we want to achieve) as well as to others. And when we display loyalty to other people, we instill a sense of trust and security in the relationship.

Respectful

This is a direct expression of having a healthy identity. When we value ourselves, we are more likely to treat everyone else with dignity. And as we've stated, everyone wants respect.

WHERE WE'RE GOING

Do you desire the same benefits of a healthy identity? Imagine realizing the impact each one would have on your life: to be fulfilled, truthful, happy, peaceful, self-controlled, friendly, caring, loyal, respected, and respectful. That reality is within our reach. We simply must not allow performance in a role to influence who we are. I acknowledge this is sometimes easier said than done, especially considering our unique upbringings and how those have shaped our lives to date.

How we grow up affects our identity. To illustrate, I'll share a bit of my own story and how it shaped me up to my early twenties.

My father was a US Marine who served in the Vietnam War. Like many other veterans of that war, he experienced great trauma. For instance, his platoon got blown up, leaving him as the lone survivor. In addition, he faced many difficult decisions in the war that haunted him for years thereafter.

He witnessed children in the villages of Vietnam being used as suicide bombers. They would approach my father with bombs strapped to their bodies. I can only imagine the inner struggle he faced in choosing his life or theirs, in one day seeing his family again or not, and in protecting his country or succumbing to the tactics of the enemy. To no surprise, these events had a major impact on the rest of his life. My father battled with post-traumatic stress disorder (PTSD) and had nearly sixty surgeries resulting from injuries sustained during the war. He eventually divorced my mother, and my childhood home was foreclosed many years later.

Now, imagine how this shaped my upbringing and the consequent impact on my identity. In no way does it compare to the trauma and pain my father experienced. I bring this up only to illustrate a point about identity and role. By the age of twenty-one, I felt a tremendous void in my self-worth. My identity was beat up. As a result, a host of bad results ensued. I spent money foolishly to fill that void, eventually leading me to bankruptcy.

I wasn't performing well in my roles. I was in a very bad place in my life. It was not until years later that I came to recognize the importance of addressing my past and its influence on who I was. By addressing my pain points, I was able to effectively separate my roles from my personal identity. If I otherwise continued to unconsciously view my identity and role as one, I surely wouldn't be writing these words today. That's because my self-concept at that time was, *I'm not worth it* and *I'm not valuable.* And when we feel this way, we tend not to invest in ourselves. Fortunately, I made radical changes that included personal development and increasing my self-value. And guess what happened? Life got better from there.

I don't know your personal story, but whatever it is, I do know we all can develop our identities to be strong, regardless of past circumstances. I urge you to look deep into how your own history has shaped your identity to date. If you uncover pain points as I did, address them. We may not realize the impact they've had on us. I certainly did not.

Furthermore, here's something even simpler you can start doing today. Let's say you rate your identity as an

"8." Start viewing it as a "10." Don't worry if you're not there yet. We'll outline steps to help reach that level. The important thing is to start thinking in this way. It will trickle down to your role, because we perform the way we feel.

And if you lead others, help them understand and develop their giftedness. When people operate in an area of giftedness, there is a greater likelihood of success. With success come positive feelings. People, in turn, perform better because how they feel inside determines how they show up outside. Remember this for yourself as well as for those you lead.

STEPS TO A HEALTHY IDENTITY

Let's keep advancing. Here are four practical steps to building a healthy identity:

Step 1—Find and Complete an Identity Assessment

Complete an assessment in the areas of self-perception, self-expression, interpersonal skills, decision-making, and stress management.

Aside from formal assessments, identify someone you trust and respect, and solicit his or her honest feedback across the same areas of focus. There's a good reason to do this. Remember the *Harvard Business Review* study on self-awareness? Even though most people believe they are self-aware, the majority are not. And for leaders who grow in seniority, there are simply fewer people above them who can provide honest feedback. Likewise, the more power a leader has, the less willing people may be to provide feedback.

Leader or not, we can counteract the lack of self-awareness by seeking frequent feedback—from bosses, peers, employees, friends, loved ones, and so on.

Step 2—Rate Yourself in Your "Role," from 1-10

Break up your role into three areas, assuming each is applicable: spouse, parent, and business leader. If one doesn't apply, swap it out for another significant role in your life such as partner, sibling, son, or daughter. How well are you doing in each role, on a scale of 1 (poor) to 10 (excellent)?

Record your rank so you may reference it later. Don't overlook this step. I encourage you to be intentionally good and record it now.

Step 3—Rate Yourself Currently in Your "Identity," from 1-10

Take time to rate your identity or self-perception of yourself (that is, who you really are at your core when you strip away titles and roles) on the same scale of 1 to 10. Record the number.

Step 4—Build a Personal Growth Plan to Grow in the Area of "Role vs Identity"

Let's say, for example, you want to grow in your role as a business leader. Build competencies aligned to your areas of strength that will benefit you in this capacity. This may include hiring coaches, reading books, or establishing and observing mentors.

As for identity, I encourage you to not only assess your giftedness but also to determine what has shaped your identity to date. When you do these things in harmony, it helps develop a clear picture of who you are and how you arrived at where you are today.

Down the road, once you've executed the plan, you'll want to review your initial rankings from steps 2 and 3.

We all start from somewhere. But wherever we begin, accept it for what it is—we can't change where we are, but we can change where we're going. This exemplifies knowing the difference between role versus identity and never confusing the two. Roles change throughout life, but identity is the one constant that can guide us toward our desired end point.

A DEFINING MOMENT

Everyone, to a degree, has a desire to develop themselves and become better. Sometimes those desires become masked or buried by thinking of role and identity as one. Roles change, but identity should not. We must develop a healthy identity that stands independent of role. Only then can our full potential come to fruition. We can all reap the rewards of becoming fulfilled, truthful, happy, peaceful, self-controlled, friendly, caring, loyal, and respectful. The sum effect will elevate us to the life design we are meant for. And it will stand as a defining moment.

7

Leadership Is Caught, Not Taught

To explain how leadership is caught but not taught, let me catch you up on how I first came to learn the importance of leadership to one's success. After all, why catch leadership if we don't understand where it can take us?

LET ME CATCH YOU UP

Back in 2003, after graduating from college, my wife and I were hustling hard to catch success. But despite all our efforts early on, we kept hitting a lid that stopped us in our tracks. It was the lid of our own leadership ability holding us back. In other words, the lid was a ceiling that was commensurate with our leadership skills. If we wanted greater success, we had to raise the lid by improving in the area of leadership. John Maxwell refers to this as "The Law of the Lid," where leadership ability determines a person's level of effectiveness.

I began to learn about and embrace this concept in 2008 when I started reading John Maxwell's books. It changed how I thought about leadership. Fast-forward to one Saturday morning in 2015. Danielle and I were on a nationwide leadership call with what used to be called The John Maxwell Team. The moderator was taking questions for John to answer live, and I decided to ask one.

"John, when you have a big dream, how do you fulfill it?"

His response was, "You need to start walking. And as you start walking, the resources, the people, and the vision start coming to fruition." This was the start of my journey with John Maxwell and how I eventually came to know that leadership is caught, not taught.

In August of 2019, Danielle and I finally attended one of John's live conferences. We weren't supposed to be there. Our plan had been to vacation in Aruba, but our expired passports had other plans. Instead, we attended a live conference in the Washington, DC, area to hear John speak. The intention was to recharge and energize ourselves with John's message, but we ended up receiving so much more. We had the opportunity to meet John in person, and he said to us, "If there's anything I can do to help you, please let me know."

Danielle and I were fortunate enough to get close to John and his team from that point forward. We gained proximity to his leadership. And let me tell you firsthand, there's something about *seeing* leadership that changes you. Personally, it gave us a new perspective. Professionally, the possibilities for what we were doing in business changed overnight. The art of the possible expanded because we were able to see what John was achieving. We found new success and eventually would come to collaborate with John and his team. What happened was really simple—we reached a new level of leadership ability because we *caught* John's leadership.

We don't need to let the lid hold us back from our potential. We all can elevate our leadership abilities. Get around leaders who are bigger, better, faster, and smarter than you are. Proximity allows you to catch their DNA. Reading books and listening to podcasts, part of being a lifelong learner, are great things to do. Over my first twenty years in business, I

> Get around great leaders, and you'll catch their DNA.

have read more than 750 books and listened to hundreds of podcasts. But one thing I can tell you is that being around John from 2019 forward has grown my leadership more than any book or podcast ever could have done. Leadership is indeed caught, not taught. It is not merely a saying; rather, it's a life walk we can all take.

As you're going on your leadership journey, surround yourself with leaders who are operating at another level. Start walking with them, and the necessary resources and skills will take shape. Do this and you'll catch their leadership DNA!

THE LEARNING PYRAMID

To elevate our leadership abilities, it's important to understand how we learn best, especially when we are around leaders. According to the learning pyramid, developed by the National Training Laboratories Institute, retention of learned knowledge varies depending on how we take in information. There are both passive and active forms of learning.[36]

Passive:

- *Lecture*, the most passive form of learning, attains 5 percent effectiveness in terms of knowledge retention. This means when someone speaks in front of an audience, 5 percent will be applied.
- *Reading*, also a passive learning method, is 10 percent effective for knowledge retention.
- *Audio/Visual* learning, another passive method, is associated with a 20 percent retention rate. This

uses elements that include visual tools such as pictures, presentations, and videos.

Now, take note of the differences below, which represent active learning methods.

Active:

- *Observation* leads to 30 percent retention. We apply 30 percent of what we observe (for example, retention through learned demonstrations such as a teacher showing students how to do something).
- *Discussion* promotes a 50 percent retention rate for learned information. And discussions promote an open exchange of ideas and viewpoints as well as self-reflection.
- *Practice* has a 75 percent rate of retention and is widely considered one of the most effective learning methods. This is where we apply what has been learned.
- *Share* what we learn, and retention jumps to 90 percent. Sharing or teaching others enhances our own knowledge because it is a reinforcing act, regardless of one's level of expertise.

Reflecting on my early experience with John, the principles of the learning pyramid were at play. What started

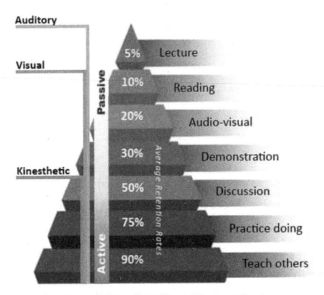

Adapted from the NTL Institute of Applied Behavioral Science Learning Pyramid

as *reading* books and listening to *audio/visuals* (recorded lessons and speeches I would find on the internet) evolved to *observation* in 2019. I observed John in his leadership environment, taking note of his actions and behavior. And whenever we had the opportunity to be with him, Danielle and I would ask him questions and *discuss* what we had observed. When we returned to our community, my team also began to *practice* what we had learned, applying the principles and techniques observed and discussed. Finally, we *shared* our newfound knowledge and empowered others to do the same. As a result, we've seen a significant positive impact—a community changed for the better.

Overall, active learning methods are more effective than passive ones. And when it comes to learning about leadership, it's not enough to simply observe. We must also discuss, practice, and share it with others. By sharing, we and others can more effectively catch leadership through the multiplication effect—because those who benefit from sharing are more likely to do the same.

It's clear that leadership is caught, not taught. As John says, "We teach what we know, but we reproduce who we are." In our case,

> *It's not enough to observe leadership. We must also discuss, practice, and share it.*

John was reproducing his leadership ability in us. It is essentially why being in the presence of great leaders can have a transformative effect on our lives. I encourage you to seek out these types of leaders, as they can raise your leadership lid to new heights.

5-STEP LEADERSHIP MENTORING

Speaking of the lid, here's what we can start doing today to raise it, tying in the learning pyramid—observation, discussion, practice, and sharing. The following five steps will appear again in this book. But for our purposes in this chapter, they are illustrated through the lens of mentorship and how I caught John Maxwell's leadership.

As John often shares, following these steps will radically change what's possible in your life and organization.[37]

Step 1—The Mentor Does It

In this step, John does it. For example, say he is leading a leadership and personal growth event that teaches his audience relevant and applicable leadership tools to take home to their communities.

Step 2—The Mentor Does It and I Am Next to Them (30 percent—Observe)

John does it, and my wife and I are next to him. We observe what John did in step 1, witnessing him directly engaging and equipping his audience to lead and create change in their lives.

Step 3—I Do It and the Mentor Is Next to Me (50 percent—Discuss)

We do it and John is next to us. Danielle and I did this with The Maxwell Leadership Foundation to drive community transformation. In the preceding step, we observed the impact John and his team were making in countries around the world and sought to do the same in the United States, starting with New York City.

In step 3, we engaged John and his team on how we can make a greater impact, one community at a time. This resulted in an initiative called Staten Island Community Transformation, where we are partnering with The Maxwell Leadership Foundation to help people learn and live good values. (To learn more about this initiative, go to www.ForStatenIsland.org.)

Step 4—I Do It (75 percent—Practice)

As coleaders of Staten Island Community Transformation, Danielle and I are now doing it. We have thousands of people experiencing transformation through transformation tables, where a peer-to-peer small group design is used for personal reflection that drives one positive weekly change among participants. Community leaders leverage our resources to participate in and deploy tables as a leadership development tool. We are finding this to be tremendously rewarding—and we are doing it in much the same way John did in steps 1 and 2.

Step 5—I Do It and Someone Else Is Next to Me (90 percent—Share)

Danielle and I do it and we bring facilitators next to us. This is multiplication. Most people stop at step 4, usually because they don't realize step 5 exists. Success may be found in step 4, but significance can only be achieved by sharing it with others. To move from success to significance, we must multiply our impact.

Variations of the five-step leadership mentoring model have been utilized by major institutions to develop their next generation of leaders. It's a highly effective method. When I do it (step 1), I am able to make a difference at an individual level. Only one person benefits. But if I do something with someone next to me, they now observe it, and we both benefit. If we discuss, practice, and share it thereafter, we create multiplication where many people benefit.

> *To move from success to significance, we must multiply our impact.*

Individuals and organizations that do this well will undoubtedly succeed for generations to come. Don't just stop at steps 2, 3, or 4. Complete all five steps as you go through the mentoring process. Step 5 will move you to significance because it changes the potential you have and the reach of your influence.

AREAS IN WHICH TO FIND MENTORS

If leadership is caught and not taught, then *how* do we choose mentors? If you're trying to determine who to get near to help yourself stretch, grow, and develop, let's return to the acronym *FISHS* from earlier in the book, summarized in brief below:

- Financial capital: your net worth
- Intellectual capital: your knowledge base
- Social capital: your relationships and network
- Human capital: your giftedness
- Spiritual capital: values you live by and traditions that define who you are

In chapter 1, we discussed this acronym in relation to building an intentional game plan and determining what to focus on. Catching leadership is no different. The five preceding categories will yield the greatest return when you intentionally develop them. And if you can catch leadership along the way, your growth will be exponential. Catching leadership in the areas of FISHS will accelerate every area of your life.

THE 3 TYPES OF MENTORS

Let's now connect the *how* with *what* types of mentors you can have. There are three types, according to John Maxwell:[38]

1. **Those who *you know* and who *know* they made a difference**. These are mentors who have made a direct impact on your life and know they helped

you. These are people you have a personal connection with or proximity to. They recognize their role as mentors to you. Through guidance, advice, or support, you catch their leadership.

2. **Those who *know you* and *didn't know* they made a difference.** These are mentors who may not have been aware of their impact on your life. They may have modeled behavior you observed and learned, for example. You may have caught a lesson from them through exposure and proximity without being consistently mentored week to week, month to month, or year to year.

3. **Those who *didn't know you* but still made a difference.** These are mentors from afar—those you never met but who still had a positive impact on your life. This includes authors, speakers, historical figures, or anyone who has influenced you without any personal connection. While not the same as direct interaction, catching leadership from afar holds great value.

MENTORS IN OUR LIVES

Are there people in your life who fall into one of these categories? I encourage you to start thinking about who is ahead of you who can serve as a mentor. No matter where we are today, each of us can benefit from being mentored.

Danielle and I are no exception. We are fortunate to have had all three types of mentors in our lives, some we knew and others we didn't. Whether each was aware of it or not, we caught their leadership, and it's the sum of what we've learned that has brought us to where we are today.

Here are just a few examples of our mentors and the leadership we caught from each:

Type 1–Those who you know and who know they made a difference

When we were starting out, our mentor was a successful businessman named Richard P., who showed us how to build a model first and relentlessly manage it thereafter. Today, Danielle and I have multiple businesses that we manage relentlessly. Each one started with building a model, from establishing our purpose, vision, and values to how we execute on our strategy.

One of our dear friends, Waikiki, illustrated to me the importance of doing for one what you would want to do for many. Even when you don't have all the resources lined up, start small and believe big. It's this lesson we caught that inspired us to create our youth leadership organization, I AM Empowering, when we initially believed we needed $30 million in funding to get started.

My friend, mentor, and pastor, Joseph (Joe) Mattera, showed me the power God has in all areas of one's life through his example. He didn't teach this to me explicitly. Instead, I learned it through observation. His actions and unwavering faith spoke louder to me than any words he could've expressed.

Rich N., a successful real estate developer and business leader, demonstrated an invaluable lesson—keep progressing and don't believe what is written about you, whether good or bad. Sometimes you will be called great, while other times you'll be torn down. When they talk good about you, you're probably not that good, and when they talk bad about you, you're probably not that bad. This lesson has enabled me to stay focused on my purpose, no matter the problem.

Another mentor is an expert and legend in the life insurance field. Richard H. is an active member of our advisory board for our generational planning firm, Wealth & Legacy Group. Through observation, he showed me the value of humility even though he is revered by so many. Seeing how humble he is has rubbed off on both Danielle and me. We try our best to catch his level of humility.

Pastor Chris Hodges (or PC, as I know him), the founder and head pastor of the second largest church in America, enlarged our vision for what it looks like to equip the next generation of leaders. It's his message that elevated our purpose for I AM Empowering—to empower youth, equip future leaders, and transform communities.

And then, of course, there is John Maxwell, who has been a lid lifter for us. John showed us what was possible because what he was doing in his mid-seventies is what we had a vision of doing in our thirties. He helped us realize that the dreams and visions in our hearts were achievable by raising our leadership ability through his example and friendship.

Type 2—Those who know you and didn't know they made a difference

Many years ago, I saw Richie M., a friend of our family, reaching remarkable heights in his business. Simply put, Richie was achieving inspiring success. Up until that point, I did not know the same was possible for Danielle and me. But I came to recognize that if he could do it, we could too. What he was doing suddenly seemed within reach. Richie was someone who walked into our lives and showed us what was possible. And he probably wasn't even aware of it at the time. Nonetheless, we caught his vision.

Type 3—Those who didn't know you but still made a difference

Ken Blanchard changed the way I lead through his book *Lead like Jesus*.[39] The book, detailing how Jesus was the best leader of all time, explains leadership through a few concepts. First, leadership is holistic, involving one's heart (motivation), head (point of view), hands (actions), and habits (daily activities). If we start with the heart, everything else follows. Second, Blanchard's four stages of leadership exemplify life as a process: novice (just starting out), apprentice (in training), journeyman (capable of working alone), and master (highly skilled and able to teach others). We have to first move from novice to apprentice before we can ever become a master.

Similarly, Rick Warren changed my life through his book *The Purpose-Driven Life*.[40] And it took no more than chapter 1, where I caught his message that "it's not about you." The purpose of life is far greater than our own personal fulfillment, peace of mind, or happiness. It's a powerful message in a self-focused world. For thirty years up to that point, I had been thinking it was all about me. But I learned that when we decide to think less about ourselves and more about others, the less prone we'll be to discouragement or disappointment. Because the purpose of our lives (and the message that God attaches to it) goes well beyond self-interest. Rick Warren set me on a purpose-driven path.

Finally, Myles Munroe shared a message I mentioned in chapter 5 that changed the course of my life. His belief that the cemetery holds all the dreams and visions people take to the grave and never accomplish unlocked great potential in me. For this reason, I want to die empty and take nothing to the grave. And I want to help others do the same. It was his message that shaped the motto Danielle and I abide by—to awaken, empower, and equip people to reach their potential. Reaching our potential ensures that potential doesn't get buried at the cemetery.

Catching leadership helps us rob the grave. It is like an outstretched arm that grabs us by the hand and pulls us toward our potential. And its grip can be powerful. But understand that it doesn't happen on its own. We don't coast to success. There has to be action behind intention. We are all capable. If we're going to grow as leaders, we need to actively develop relationships with people, read books, listen to podcasts, and catch what leaders say and do.

> *Catching leadership helps us rob the grave.*

5 GOOD STEPS TO CATCH LEADERSHIP

No one catches leadership by accident. After all, it is not enough to say we want to grow. This is simply having good intentions. Good intentions require action—this is being intentionally good. That's why now I'm going to turn to good actions you can take to catch the leadership of others. I encourage you to take note of the following five actions and your responses as you read along.

Step 1—Make a list of those mentors who you know and who know they made a difference.

Take a moment to reflect on the mentors who have made a real difference in your life. Write down their names and the qualities they possess that you admire. These are mentors who you personally know and know they made a difference in your life.

Step 2—Make a list of those mentors who know you and didn't know they made a difference.

Acknowledge those who have made a difference, even if they are unaware. Take a minute or two to write down the names of mentors who don't know they have influenced you. Yes, they may not realize it, but they have helped shape who you are today. If possible, consider reaching out to thank them and express your gratitude.

Step 3—Make a list of those mentors who didn't know you and yet made a difference.

These are people who have impacted you from afar. For me, it was Ken Blanchard, Rick Warren, and Myles Munroe. I haven't met Ken or Rick yet, but I will. And unfortunately, I won't have the pleasure of meeting Myles, as he's no longer with us. Make a similar list for yourself, keeping in mind books read or podcasts listened to.

Steps 1, 2, and 3 are essential, because they help us identify and appreciate the mentors who have shaped our lives, both directly and indirectly. Reflecting on these individuals provides clarity on not only the qualities we admire in each but also what we may seek out from future mentors in subsequent steps.

Step 4—Make a list of one to three people who you plan to mentor.

Choose to mentor those who may be a little behind you, individuals you can help get where they want to go. The great thing is, it doesn't matter where you are in your career. Whether you just started or are at the end of a long career, it's all relative to the mentee.

Step 5—Make a list of one to three people who you are going to ask to mentor you.

If you've chosen to invest in others (step 4), then you've likewise earned the right to ask others to invest in you. Put a list together of one to three people who you are going to ask to personally mentor you. Consider the FISHS acronym described earlier when you're creating your list. I would place emphasis on social capital or the relationships and network you have. I'm a big believer that our social network influences our net worth. Find people who are really good at building relationships and strong networks of contacts. They will be the same people you catch leadership from.

Steps 4 and 5 are all about intentionality and future planning. Step 4 specifically helps us develop a mindset of service. I believe that if we want mentors to come into our lives, then we need to mentor others first. Said differently, once we plan to mentor someone, the right mentor comes when the mentee is ready.

Think of mentorship as a river. Just like a river flows with life, so can you in mentoring people. But a lack of mentorship, whether you're the mentor or mentee, stagnates life in the same way a reservoir lacks flow. We need mentorship because it creates life—when it flows *from* us, it also flows *to* us.

> *If we want mentors to come into our lives, then we need to mentor others first.*

This sets you up for step 5, which is of equal importance. It is here that we seek out guidance and support from those who have more experience or expertise in areas we want to grow (FISHS). The mentors we choose from this point forward will enable us to accelerate our growth because we will have the opportunity to catch their leadership.

SMART AND HEART

When it comes to leadership, most people think it comes down to being smart. You do have to be smart; there's no doubt about it. But you also have to have heart. Smart plus heart equals effectiveness. Heart is all about people. For many years, I put my vision above people. But with time, maturity, and some bumps and bruises along the way, it became clear there is no vision without the people. You don't accomplish a vision without the help of others. The lid cannot be raised alone. We need to elevate our abilities by catching leadership from people. Start to raise that lid with others today. Be a mentor to people, seek mentors for yourself, and follow the five steps to catching leadership. After all, leadership is not meant to just be observed. It should be discussed, practiced, and shared with others. And when we do this well, we can also multiply our impact and move from success to significance.

8

Getting a Return on Your Failures

Most people want to get a return on their investment, but how many people actually want to get a return on their failures? Who wants failure in the first place?

A ROCKY PATH

I have failed often over my lifetime, particularly between the ages of eighteen and twenty-one years old. I have so many stories of failure that it would probably blow your mind. For better or worse, failure is part of life, especially for those looking to achieve success. Just consider the following story, which is so remarkable that it has been told countless times and in countless ways:

Born in 1946, a man arrived in New York City in 1969 to pursue his dream of being an actor. However, all he seemed to face was rejection, failure, and a string of people telling him no—that he talked funny, walked funny, and couldn't act.

As a struggling actor, he was forced to sell his dog for twenty-five dollars just to pay his electric bill. He was rejected approximately fifteen hundred times by talent scouts, agents, and everyone in the film industry. He was often broke and at times homeless, living and sleeping in the New Jersey Port Authority bus terminal for three weeks while trying to scrape together money for another apartment.

At several points in his early career, he considered quitting. But he kept pursuing his dream, gradually finding work as an extra in films alongside doing odd jobs, and eventually writing a screenplay that garnered the interest of Hollywood studios. His big break was an offer to purchase the script for as much as $325,000, with one condition— he did not star in the film. But instead of abandoning his dream, the man rejected the offer. He eventually accepted just $35,000 and a percentage of future sales in order to also be the lead actor in the film.

What happened next is literally a page out of a Hollywood success story. The film grossed $225 million in 1976. In addition, the man was nominated for ten Oscars, including Best Actor and Best Original Screenplay at the 49th Academy Awards in 1977. The film also won the Academy Awards for Best Picture, Best Directing, and

Best Film Editing. Since this time, the man went on to become a critically acclaimed actor whose films have collectively grossed $4 billion to date.

You may have guessed that this is the remarkable story of Sylvester Stallone and his film *Rocky*.[41]

The best leaders—those who do anything of significance—face failure head-on. When, not if, they fail, those individuals keep moving forward anyway. It's the difference in the lives of those who achieve success. And it's what enabled Stallone to go on to box-office fame and produce a multi-billion-dollar brand despite failing fifteen hundred times prior.

Anyone who does anything of significance faces failure head-on.

OUR RELATIONSHIP WITH FAILURE

Fear of failure is real. Consider that of 1,083 American adults surveyed, 31 percent, nearly one in every three, reported being afraid of failure, according to a social network survey in 2015.[42] More so, 90 percent of CEOs surveyed in 2018 admitted that failure was their main cause of distress.[43] Failure has become too personal. When something goes wrong, we default to asking *who is to blame* instead of *what went wrong*.

Failure gets wrapped up too much in one's identity. As a result, we often try to avoid failure in a variety of ways:

- delaying action due to uncertainty (hesitating);
- avoiding doing anything new (sticking with familiar routines);
- setting low expectations for success in a given task or initiative (aiming low);
- developing last-minute issues (making excuses);
- deferring action without good reason, even when it can greatly improve one's life (acting passive);
- always taking the path of least resistance (choosing convenience over growth);
- underselling our capabilities (self-sabotage); and
- outright procrastinating (dragging one's feet).

To get a return, we must have a healthy relationship with failure. Take it from some of the world's most renowned industry leaders. Steve Jobs, ousted eight years after founding the technology company Apple, once said, "I didn't see it then, but it turned out that getting fired from Apple was the best thing that could have ever happened to me."[44]

Reflect on that statement for a moment. A visionary in the field of personal computers and telecommunications, including revolutionary products such as the iPhone, Jobs recognized his best lesson came from failure.

Bill Gates, cofounder of Microsoft and one of the wealthiest people in the world, says, "It's fine to celebrate success but it is more important to heed the lessons of failure."[45]

John Maxwell says, "The difference between average people and achieving people is their perception of and their response to failure."[46] How we respond counts most.

And finally, the great scientist Albert Einstein is credited with saying, "Failure is success in progress."

There are two takeaways from these examples:

1. Everyone fails.
2. There's something to learn from each failure.

Simply put, failure is the best friend of success when we embrace it and learn from it. This is *successfully failing*, and it requires shifting away from old beliefs and identifying the lessons in life's shortcomings.

If you don't have a healthy relationship with failure today, that's okay. I didn't always have a healthy relationship with failure either. The shift happened for me many years ago when a coach said, "At the end of the day, reflect and write your lessons learned." The exercise was powerful because it conditioned me to learn a daily lesson, even if I wasn't happy about

> *Failure is the best friend of success when we embrace it and learn from it.*

what had happened. And if we stay disciplined, we'll get better at it.

THE CYCLE OF SUCCESS

Documenting the lesson learned puts us in position to improve. But it is not enough on its own. There's a formula by John Maxwell I introduced in chapter 1 called the cycle of success:

Test—Fail—Learn—Improve—Reenter

When—not *if*—we fail, why not do it successfully? By following this formula, we can ensure a return on our failures. Test and identify what works, fail in what doesn't, learn from it, improve, and get back in the game tomorrow. To intentionally move through the cycle of success, we must understand its parts.

Part 1—Test

Vision Is a Prerequisite

We saw in chapter 5 that great commitments precede great achievements. Testing is part 1 of committing. It can be uncomfortable at first because of the fear of failure. The fastest way to overcome this is to have a vision—let's call it a prerequisite. It's the first thing I teach leaders around the world to do.

If we don't have a vision, we're less likely to step out of our comfort zone and test. But when we have a strong vision, it pulls us forward. We're more willing to step out and test in pursuit of a vision that is bright. Consider the opposite. What incentive is there to test and possibly fail if we can't see what we're pursuing?

No One Is Good Their First Time

Today, I communicate for a living. But in the early stages of my career, I struggled with shaky communication. Picture this: profuse sweating, choking on my words, and feelings of sheer embarrassment.

No, I'm not talking about my first time speaking onstage. All this actually describes my first sales experience with two clients in my early twenties. They took pity on me, giving me a cup of water and placing a cold rag on my face to cool down. I tested and failed miserably that day. But I pressed on. Even though I was terrified, I got up, tested again, got a little better, and came back for more.

Perfection is elusive in an imperfect world. As a recovering perfectionist myself, understanding this fact is liberating. We are not going to be good the first time around.

If we accept that and intentionally test with this in mind, everything becomes easier from there. Know that growth and improvement will come from the process of testing. And each day is an opportunity to test anew.

Patience Is a Must

If we are going to reap rewards from our failures, we must be patient. Through patience, we come to understand that success is a journey; it's not achieved overnight. Real transformation unfolds gradually. If we test and are patient, we put ourselves in position to win—to get a return on our failures.

Persistence Is Required

When the 2020 COVID-19 pandemic started, I was tired and drained. If there were ever an excuse to take the foot off the gas, this was it. I remember Danielle saying, "We can't stop right now. People need us now more than ever." We pressed forward, even though things around us were discouraging.

Are there areas of your life where you feel like giving up? Whatever the challenge, I encourage you to keep moving forward. If we are going to realize a return on failure, we have to persist. Even when times are tough, we cannot succumb to fatigue or pressure.

Your Future Must Always Be Brighter Than Your Past

Imagine a company launching a new product model that is less impressive, less advanced, and less appealing than its predecessors. How do you think that would fare in the market? If you wouldn't invest in a new car or phone that comes with downgrades, why should you settle for a future of lesser quality compared to the present?

Don't settle for less; have a future that is brighter than your past. Believe in its truth for your life and consider it nonnegotiable. This is a prerequisite in the same way as vision. It has the power to amplify the cycle of success, pulling you forward. Without it, you're not going to be patient and persistent enough to reenter and test.

A brighter future shapes vision, reinforces patience, and fuels persistence to keep testing.

Consider if the past is brighter. What incentive is there to test and possibly fail for a bleak outlook? It's quite simple: a brighter future shapes vision, reinforces patience, and fuels persistence to keep testing.

KEY QUESTION: Are you willing to "test" in each area of life, such as your business, career, and relationships?

Where are you willing to go? Testing can be uncomfortable, as it brings the risk of failure. However, if we embrace the notion of failing, testing is more manageable. Even if things don't work out, we become more willing to try again. Failure is now just a temporary setback, not the end of the road.

Part 2—Fail

Success and Failure Are Best Friends

As I mentioned earlier, we must have a healthy relationship with failure. To embrace the losses as they come, we have to understand that success and failure are best friends. We don't have success without failure.

I avoided facing my failures for many years. I associated them with my identity. Failing was an indictment of my abilities as a person. This was self-sabotage. In the same way, most people separate success from failure. But that separation creates limitation. There's no room for learning a lesson, improving, reentering, and getting a return on failure with that type of thought process.

How Fear of Failure Develops

How does fear of failure develop? I used the example of a garage door earlier in the book. From birth to ten years old, our garage door is fully open. These are the most impressionable years of one's life. From ages eleven through thirty, the garage door shuts halfway. Now, only some things come in, while others don't. After thirty years old, it becomes difficult to change accumulated belief systems. What's more, belief systems drive behavior, and behavior creates results.

If we're going to embrace failure, we have to address how the fear of failure developed in our lives. As children, we were likely taught not to fail. I know I was taught to avoid failure, particularly during the period when the garage door was wide-open. The notion of "make Mom and Dad proud," which is a great thing, became entangled in not trying difficult things, because if I failed, I ran the risk of embarrassing my parents. Understanding this was the first step to intentionally changing my own belief system.

How the fear of failure developed in your own life defines how much you're willing to test and potentially fail. Take the time to identify how fear of failure developed in your life. The garage door is closing, yes. But if you are intentional in not only understanding but also changing your current belief system, there is success beyond the door.

Failure Is an Event, Not a Person

Failure is an event. It's not a person. When we fail, it doesn't mean *we* are failures. Instead, the *event* was a failure. What we did at that moment simply did not work.

Fail is indeed part 2 in our formula, the cycle of success. But it shows up everywhere because it's best friends with success. If success and failure are connected, how can failure possibly be identity in isolation? Failure is merely the event at a moment in time that brings us closer to success.

Let's take a closer look at our formula once more:

$$Test—Fail—Learn—Improve—$$
$$Reenter = Cycle\ of\ Success$$

And keep in mind:

- Failing is an event.
- Events lead to learning, because there's a lesson in everything.
- The more events, the more learning that can occur.
- Learning improves us.
- Greater improvement means greater probability of future success.
- Therefore, failure and success are best friends.

None of this holds true if failure is anything else but an event. And if there's one thing you can trust, it's this: there are no false statements in our equation. We need the events to learn and improve so we can win upon reentry.

Failure is merely the event at a moment in time that brings us closer to success.

Failure Is a Treasure Trove of Wealth

Failure is a treasure—a precious chest awaiting discovery. When we embrace failure, we gain access to the key that unlocks the treasure chest's hidden riches. If we treat it as anything other than a treasure, we may never see the wealth that it stores. The treasure chest stays locked forever.

Unfortunately, so many people don't want to look at what's inside the treasure chest. Why? Fear of failure. Yet the true failure lies in not recognizing that we maximize the treasure trove of wealth by drawing from success and failure alike.

Failure Is a Great Teacher

If we look at failure as a teacher or educator, then we always ask what can be learned from the event and how we can grow from here. If we don't look at failure as a great teacher, then we're going to see it as a great disciplinarian. We'll look to avoid it, missing out on the cycle of success.

KEY QUESTION: What is Your Perspective of Failure?

Do you fear failure? Is failing something you avoid altogether? The truth is, we can't get a return on failure if we otherwise don't embrace it. And embracing failure is difficult if we separate it from success. Look at failure through a different lens. Recognize that failure is an integral part of the cycle of success. It is tied to, and not distinct from, success. Therefore, great leaders figure out how to get a return on their failures.

Part 3—Learn

We Live in a School Called *Life*

A coach once shared his personal motto with me, which was very simple yet powerful: "We live in a school called *life*." When we don't look at life as a school, then whatever happens defines us. But if we have the perspective that everything in life is a school, then whatever happens is now a learning event. We can assess what happens, learn from it, improve, and reenter.

Every Person and Event Contains a Valuable Lesson

The same coach also taught me that every person and event contains a valuable lesson. If life is the school, then people and events are the faculty that educate us within that construct. The key is learning. Try to learn something from everyone and everything. Recognize the lessons beneath the surface of people and events.

Lessons You Resist Will Persist

It's okay to fail, but we must learn from it. In the early part of my career, I used to not learn from failure. Instead, I figured, *I'll just run through the wall.* I learned the hard way that if you don't learn the lesson, eventually the wall will get the best of you.

Consider how much easier it is to climb over the wall. Or to walk around the wall. Better yet, how about not even going near the wall anymore? That's what failure and learning are all about. If the wall symbolizes failure, we'll keep hitting it until we learn the lesson. The lesson, however, changes our behavior. It enables us to get over, around, or nowhere near failure. But if we resist the lesson, we'll keep hitting the wall.

A Lesson Will Be Repeated, Until Learned

To learn the lesson, start by asking why failure is occurring and what can be learned from it. For example, the wall that held back one of my companies was the lid on my leadership ability. Although my vision was high, my leadership was low. I was continuously hitting the lid because I was repeating the same lesson. Things did not change until I finally learned the lesson.

Every Time a Lesson Is Repeated, It Becomes More Painful

Are you choosing the cycle of pain over success? Most people do. They test, fail, and reenter. This is simply getting back in the game with the same mindset that created the failure. Consider the cycle of success once more. If we were to take "learn" out of the formula, there is also no "improve." What happens now? We test, fail, and reenter over and over again. There is no return on our failures.

Test—Fail—Reenter = Cycle of Pain

The cycle of pain converts to success when we add learning. It is learning that creates the improvement needed to reenter successfully. Otherwise, lessons we do not embrace and learn from will keep repeating, with each occurrence more painful than the last.

KEY QUESTION: What lesson have you repeated?

KEY PRINCIPLES: We live in a school called *life*. Every person and event, teachers of the school, contains a valuable lesson. The lessons you resist will persist. A lesson will be repeated until learned. Every time a lesson is repeated, it becomes more painful.

What lessons have you not learned that keep repeating with increasing pain? Lessons we resist and repeat become more painful for a variety of reasons. For one, there is opportunity cost in time lost to repeated errors. Our confidence also begins to erode as each mistake chips away at our self-belief. A mistake, the thing that is hurting us, compounds as well. Lastly, the emotional impact (disappointment) intensifies over time.

We can break away from the pain by learning the lesson. I encourage you to test, fail, learn, improve, and reenter. That's how you get a return on your failures. It enables us to achieve our vision, experience career growth, and create a better business, family, and life overall.

Part 4—Improve

Let's now equip ourselves to reach our potential by improving after failure. One tool to do so is through a key acronym described earlier and originally taught by John Maxwell. To intentionally improve, we must PLAN AHEAD.

P—Predetermine What a Win Looks Like

In order to improve, we have to clearly define what winning looks like. I work with so many organizations that show up every day but haven't defined what a win is. By not defining what a win looks like, we blur the difference between failure and success. And if we can't recognize failure, we also can't get a return on it.

L—Lay Out Your Goals

Once we know what a win looks like, we need to set specific, measurable, realistic, and time-bound goals aligning to it. As a business leader, this may mean reaching a certain number of new clients, appointments, and/or other milestones. Hitting or missing on our goals clarifies if we are on track to win.

A—Adjust Your Priorities

Laying out a set of goals allows for adjustments. This is where most leaders struggle. To accomplish anything, we need to prioritize—the answer to everything cannot be yes. We have to push back on certain things, say no to people, and take some meetings off our calendars in favor of others. Adjusting priorities requires daily discipline, but it comes with long-term payoffs.

N—Notify Key Team Members

Notify important people, including those on your team as well as family members. Let them know the direction of travel. They help us to navigate.

When I realized that my leadership lid was low, I told my wife I was going to invest in developing my leadership

GETTING A RETURN ON YOUR FAILURES

ability. Notifying her was important. It kept me accountable while also providing her advance notice on how this decision would affect our life.

A—Allow Time for Acceptance

Before testing or reentering in pursuit of winning, we need to allow time for acceptance.

One of the things many leaders often do poorly is not allow sufficient time for acceptance of goals or priorities. I used to do this poorly. I would define the win, lay out a set of goals, and identify my priorities. Immediately after notifying key personnel, I'd tell the team to head into action. I may have spent anywhere from ten to thirty hours charting the course but only provided minutes for the team to get on board. It's like running a relay race—we are halfway down the track already, but our teammates are at the starting line. We must allow others to catch up to where we are.

H—Head into Action

This is the part that most people and organizations do well. They put a checklist together of all tasks that need to be done and take action.

Consider how that checklist looks if we don't start by predetermining what a win looks like.

E—Expect Problems

Whether or not we want to accept it, problems are going to occur. If we are trying to achieve anything of significance, it would serve us well to expect and try to get ahead of problems. Doing so will make all the difference in the world. Yes, we may still fail regardless. But the failure will allow us to better anticipate problems next time (when we reenter).

A—Always Point to Successes

Our key team members, family members, or any other important people who are along for the journey need to win. They are the events along the path to achievement. How do we stay on course? Point to the successes, as success fans the flames for greater achievement. We need to celebrate them in the same way a fire needs to be supplied with oxygen.

D—Daily Review Your Progress

When we review our progress every day, we increase the probability of getting to where we want to go. As previously mentioned, we are on a journey. Make it a habit to assess progress along the path to achievement. Schedule time in your calendar or daily planner to do this. It helps determine if we're on track or if adjustments are needed.

KEY QUESTION: Where is a PLAN AHEAD needed in your life?

Are there areas of your life that have not been working or need improvement? I challenge you to examine each area of your life for opportunities to improve. The better we are at doing this, the greater the potential upside. Because if we can identify more, we can repeatedly address and improve more with the PLAN AHEAD tool. We can get a return on failure every time.

Part 5—Reenter

New Mindset Is Required

The Bible says that new wine is for fresh wineskins: "No one pours new wine into old wineskins. Otherwise, the wine will burst the skins, and both the wine and the wineskins will be ruined."[47] This short statement applies to mindset in much the

> *An old mindset can't take us where we want to go.*

same way. To reenter, we have to understand that an old mindset can't take us where we want to go, just like an old wineskin can't support new wine. The old mindset has limitations. In order to succeed, we need a new mindset.

New Belief Systems Are Required

A new mindset will create new belief systems, because what we put in our minds creates our beliefs. Belief systems, as mentioned, call for intentionality. As we reenter, the right belief system will support where we want to go. Make an intentional effort to revisit and redesign your belief systems to be in alignment with a renewed mindset.

New Behaviors Are Required

Beliefs turn into behaviors, and behaviors create the results in our lives. To reenter, we need new behaviors that support where we want to go and what we want to accomplish.

New Strategies Are Required

As you can see, we are moving in sequential order, with each tenet of reentering connected to another. In following suit, beliefs and strategy should be in unity. If you're reentering, get a new strategy since the old one tested and failed.

It is often said that your network equals and/or improves your net worth. Who in your network can help you with a new strategy? Are there individuals who you can lean on for wisdom? Don't just rely on yourself. If you don't have a good network, take the time to develop one. A good network will translate into overall success because you'll have access to people who can direct you to the right strategy.

KEY QUESTION: When should you reenter?

When you get knocked down and fail, take some time to get up so you can learn from the knockdown. Don't just jump right up. Yes, timing is key. We need to reenter at the right time. But we also need to have a great idea or strategy.

A lot of times, people jump up after failure because they're embarrassed. But I encourage you to stay down for a little bit and learn why you failed. This will help you recognize who to consult with or lean on.

EMBRACE FAILURE

As you continue on your leadership journey, I encourage you to embrace failure. It's not that failure is altogether bad. It's the fear of failure that is bad. Fear stops us from testing and limits our growth. Recognize that failure and success are best friends, overcome the fear, and enter the cycle of success: *test, fail, learn, improve, and reenter stronger*. Seek good counsel and perfect the timing of reentry. If you do this in every area of your life and it becomes a habit, I can assure you that your future will always be brighter than your past. You will get a return on your failures. And as the cycle of success unfolds, it will result in realization of the dreams and visions rooted in your heart.

Learn, Earn, and Return

Learn, Earn, and Return is a process I have embraced in my life. It is a great enabler to achieving anything of significance.

AN INTENTIONAL PROCESS

Let's break it down in simple terms. *Learning* is the foundation of personal and professional growth. We must continuously learn to grow. Learning puts us in a position to *earn* a livelihood. Greater investment in learning will raise our earning ability and potential. *Return* is about using your collective experience through learning and earning to benefit others. The resources you've earned put you in a prime position to give back to others. Giving back is key to making a difference in the world and leaving behind a meaningful legacy.

I honestly did not always see things this way. During my first ten years in business, I wanted to earn before I truly learned my craft. In other words, I wanted the market to pay me more than I was worth at the time. Due to a scarcity belief system and mindset, my earnings potential was capped. This was completely self-inflicted.

Reversing the order of Learn and Earn also unintentionally shut the proverbial door to new opportunities. Let's put the situation I'm describing in perspective. I placed a ceiling on what I was worth to the market and had little to no momentum behind me. These two limiting forces had momentum working against me, making my situation seem worse than it was.

Momentum is life's great exaggerator.

During this early part of my career, I also had an unrealistic expectation for how much I could deliver in a short period of time. I tended to pack things in, thinking I had only a year or two. If only I could get more done in that time, I would achieve my goals. I failed to realize that was unrealistic. As I've mentioned earlier, we overestimate what we can accomplish in a day and underestimate what we can accomplish in a lifetime. My approach to tasks created a false expectation that set me up for disappointment. It was overwhelming and frustrating.

Fortunately, I came to recognize the value in accomplishing more over a lifetime. If I could break a lifetime down in a manageable way, it became clear that our dream would become a reality over time. That's why understanding each of these three phases—Learn, Earn, and Return—is essential to accomplishing anything in life. Following this phased approach will also build tremendous momentum in your life. This is where momentum's power will be exaggerated in your favor. When you have it, your situation will seem better than it is. If you can shift momentum in your favor, you can accomplish amazing things.

To best illustrate how Learn, Earn, and Return works, here's how it has applied to my life:

1. The *Learn* Phase: Ages twenty-one to forty years old. During this time, I invested in my own personal development. I built the habits of becoming a lifelong learner.

2. The *Earn* Phase: Ages forty-one to sixty years old. During these years, which I am currently in, the accumulation of skills and experience has positioned Danielle and me to achieve the dreams that have been deposited in our hearts.

3. The *Return* Phase: Ages sixty-one to when God calls me home. During this period, I expect to utilize

our FISHS priorities to make the greatest impact. A greater amount of effort will be devoted to leaving a legacy of significance for future generations.

Are the age ranges for Learn, Earn, and Return set in stone? Absolutely not. The process does not apply to everyone in the same way. This represents my unique journey, which is not a one-size-fits-all path. There are countless ways the journey can vary. Many people, including myself, will continue to acquire new skills throughout their lives. The Learn and Earn phases may be experienced simultaneously, sometimes out of necessity. There may also be planned and unplanned breaks in the workforce. No matter how different your journey is, embracing this approach puts things in perspective and can change the course of your life.

THE LEARN PHASE

Zig Ziglar famously said, "Success is the maximum utilization of the ability that you have."[48] Most people don't maximize their ability. The Learn phase is all about addressing this.

Learning maximization is critical to building momentum that transitions you into the Earn phase of your life. One of the best ways to accomplish this is through mentors. Mentors are life's great accelerators. They help bring out your hidden potential.

Most people recognize the value of mentors, yet most still do not have one. According to research conducted by Olivet Nazarene University in 2019, 76 percent of people surveyed thought mentors were important, but only 37 percent had one at the time of the study. Those with mentors identified as being

Mentors are life's great accelerators.

happier in their current jobs than those without a mentor. Lastly, 14 percent of mentor relationships were started by the mentee, relative to 61 percent of those relationships developing naturally.[49]

If you're wondering how to get a mentor, my personal advice is to apply a simple principle: ask and you shall receive.[50]

I encourage you to be part of the 37 percent who ask for mentors. They can give you a significant head start in the Learn phase of your life. For this reason, I have had mentors to help me learn and grow. However, simply asking for a mentor is not enough. To help you be intentional in aligning with the *right* mentors, let's utilize the FISHS methodology.

FISHS: LET'S SWIM DEEP

Whether you're developing an intentional game plan (chapter 1) or getting around leaders (chapter 7) and mentors alike, developing in these categories leads to the greatest success.

#1—Financial Capital

This is all about your net worth. We need mentors to help us develop our assets and grow our net worth, whether through real estate, the markets, or other avenues. Identifying a financial mentor will help you grow in this area of your personal and business life.

Any mentor worth his or her salt will agree that you should always live on less than you earn. It's a simple process, yet most of us don't apply it in practice. If you make $100,000, live on less than that amount. If you make $250,000, live on less than that, and so forth. Live on less than you make. Doing that exponentially increases the odds you will succeed over long periods of time throughout the Learn, Earn, and Return phases.

It is also important to build a financial buffer or security blanket. I didn't do this in the early part of my career. As a result, I felt a tremendous unhealthy pressure to perform.

Please build a security blanket of six to twelve months' worth of living expenses that you set aside. What does this do for you? It will help ease any unpredictable bumps in the road. It gives you flexibility. It makes it easier to make important decisions. In general, most people are probably one bad decision away from going bankrupt. How do I know? Because I went bankrupt at age twenty-one. In the early part of my career, I didn't have that buffer. I also did not initially learn and get a return on my failures. If you have a security blanket, you can make better decisions and stay on track to accomplish your vision.

If you choose the right mentors in this area, you will likely find that each of them has implemented disciplines to succeed.

#2—Intellectual Capital

Mentors will help you find the right resources to help grow your IQ. These may include books, podcasts, seminars, and/or events. An important element of this area comes back to intentionality. Target areas of strength, which will in turn allow you to learn far faster than if you were trying to develop a weakness. As we've seen, our weaknesses on average will get us to a knowledge base of good. But in targeting our strengths, we are more likely to get to excellence.

If you are uncertain about your strengths, there are scientifically proven assessments that can be a big help. I would also consider assessing your strengths and weaknesses through observation. If I spent time observing you every day, it would likely take me months or, in some cases, years to determine what these are. In contrast, assessments get to the science quickly. This is precisely why so many exist in the area of leadership and development.

Generally, assessments utilize a series of questions to reveal the presence of skills and strengths that can aid you in growing quicker. I use them at my leadership coaching company, Lions Pride Leadership.

Knowing your strengths is likewise beneficial to your mentors. Keeping you focused on your areas of strength will provide valuable feedback and support to help you become more creative and successful.

#3—Social Capital

This is about your relationships and networks. I admittedly struggled with this in the early part of my Learn phase. Since my emotional intelligence was rather low, I did not know how to best connect with people and build solid relationships. That said, there are some who are socially gifted. It just never came naturally to me until I reached my late thirties.

Mentors can play an instrumental role here. Mentors who have demonstrated an understanding of the dynamics tied to relationships can be invaluable to your development. They can help you navigate social situations and cultivate emotional intelligence as well as interpersonal skills to help you build meaningful connections with others. Mentors can also make introductions to new people and open doors that would have otherwise taken a lifetime to open.

Developing socially is going to force you to be selective in terms of who you let into your circle. Having proximity to the right mentors radically expedites your vision and life. This is referred to as the *proximity effect*. As Jim Rohn famously said, "You are the average of the five people you spend the most time with."[51] For this reason, I carefully determine who I am going to ask to mentor me, a process I revisit every year.

I also identify who I am going to serve each year. Serving mentors is really important because it helps them while providing you with proximity. So, if you're in your Learn phase, find people who are further ahead of you and serve them. Serving allows for observing. You can say, "I don't want anything but to help," or, "Let me add value to your life." You can add, "You don't have to pay me. I just want to be around you and learn from you."

> Serving allows for observing.

From the perspective of a mentor, I also pick a small group of people every December who I want to intentionally invest in. Looking toward December of the following year, I ask myself a few questions:

- What was the fruit of my investment?
- Who did my mentees impact?
- Did they bear fruit?

If someone mentors you, make sure they get a great return on their investment. It doesn't always have to be financial, but strive to make sure the mentor gets something valuable out of the relationship.

#4—Human Capital

Human capital is all about your leadership ability. The good thing about leadership ability is that you can always grow it, regardless of your starting point. This comes down to the attitude you have every day, which is a choice you can consciously make.

Attitude is a key factor influencing your human capital and leadership ability. Two other factors include your emotional quotient (EQ) and natural giftedness. EQ is your ability to understand and manage your own emotions as well as the emotions of others. This goes hand in hand with effective communication and leadership.

The right attitude primes you for increasing emotional intelligence as well as tapping into your giftedness.

Giftedness is the thing you do well, your unique skills and abilities that you bring to the world. I am a big believer that a person's giftedness opens doors to opportunities and puts them in the presence of influential people.

Let's put it all together. The right attitude primes you for increasing emotional intelligence as well as tapping into your giftedness.

If you are in the learning years of your life, I encourage you to read at minimum one book a month. Just read one book that will grow you as a leader, increase your emotional intelligence, and refine your giftedness. There's no right or wrong book as long as you are intentional about the areas you want to grow in.

Every month, I choose a book that helps me become an effective man of God, husband, business leader, and communicator. I develop myself intentionally every month, year in and year out. I want people to know and experience that there's something different about me. Be intentional in how you develop yourself. The rewards are tremendous!

Take the time to also understand your giftedness: mission, competency, and style. It is the unique combination of these three that sets you apart.

When you not only understand but also develop, grow, and nurture your giftedness, you become more valuable to those around you.

If we take the time to refine our gift during our learning years, we become more valuable to others and the market. People will find you and pay you for it, regardless of the field you're in (technology, leadership, math, accounting). Don't worry about getting paid immediately.

Remember, refining our gifts takes time, effort, and intentionality. But the rewards are well worth it. If you refine it first and make that a continual process, you will become more valuable in all areas of your life.

#5–Spiritual

Spiritual in this context is meant to reflect the values you live by and the traditions that define who you are. Values and traditions are important to establish during the Learn phase. They help you navigate the world, governing actions that ultimately result in the quality of your life.

Let's take a moment to look at both values and traditions in a bit more detail.

Values

Personally and professionally, Danielle and I apply a set of values that we reference by using the acronym LISTENS:

- Lifelong learner: This first value is all about developing and growing, being better than we were the day before. As we embrace the cycle of success (test, fail, learn, improve, and reenter), we become lifelong learners.
- Intentional: This means acting with purpose. I want to be intentional with how I grow. I want

to be intentional with who I help develop. I want to be intentional with how I make a difference in everything that I do. Intentionality is a choice, not a by-product of something else.

- **S**tewardship: This is when I use time and resources wisely, making good decisions for the long-term success of those around me. I want to be a good steward of the resources entrusted to me.
- **T**eamwork: This is working together with others toward common goals. I want to be a good team member, player, and partner.
- **E**xcellence: I want and strive for excellence in all I do. Perfection is not possible in an imperfect world.
- **N**onattachment: I give my best while not being attached to the outcome, being fully present in the moment.
- **S**implicity: This means to take complexity and narrow it down to make things as simple as possible.

This last value was recently added after eight years—specifically because of the times we are living in today. In a world that continues to grow in complexity, I want my personal life and business affairs to be simple. Simplicity is very attractive. When you can take complexity and make it very simple, people want to know who you are and what you do.

Another value I want to highlight from my list is excellence. As I write this book in 2023, we are living in a world where most people are giving as little as possible but want to be paid as much as possible. I don't see this trend changing. In fact, it is more profound today than it has been in the last twenty years of my life. If you truly want to differentiate yourself, do things with excellence and give more than you take. If you commit to excellence, your career will go to new heights. The gap between where you are versus where others are will be tremendous. And when opportunities come, they will be given to you.

People tend to think opportunities are luck. But they are almost always the result of disciplined, consistent behavior. The best way to anchor to such behaviors is through learning and living good values.

Whatever values you decide to focus on, ensure they are ones you won't compromise. I've shared the ones that I live by both personally and professionally. I'm a big believer that I am who I am, everywhere I am. I don't want to be one person when I'm with friends, another person when I'm working, and yet another when I'm with my wife. Values allow me to be the same person everywhere I am, regardless of who I am with. Build values into your life as you continue to grow in leadership and influence.

Traditions

This is a straightforward subject, so I'll keep it brief. Stated simply, traditions help you keep what's most important to your family. Traditions I keep include how my family celebrates Easter, Thanksgiving, and Christmas. There are other traditions that are special and specific just to me and my family. Is it important to be very successful financially but lose every relationship? Or is it better to learn how to value and appreciate your family? I trust you choose the latter.

It is important to learn how to value people, to develop and appreciate them as you grow. Recently, my mother came close to death twice. The experience taught me to not only appreciate life in a new way but also to truly be present with and value her. I now take every day with her as a gift, whereas I previously expected each day. It is a newfound tradition that allows me to honor and celebrate my mother with a renewed mind.

Whether it's a holiday gathering or quality time shared over a meal, traditions play an important role in shaping your life. They provide a sense of stability and fulfillment. So be sure to establish and keep traditions. Your family is counting on you.

THE LEARN PHASE IN A NUTSHELL

In the Learn phase, develop yourself in the five areas of FISHS: financial, intellectual, social, human, and spiritual.

Next, clarify your values. Have a clear understanding of what you value and will be governed by. Mine are LISTENS: lifelong learner, intentional, stewardship, teamwork, excellence, non-attachment, and simplicity.

Last, look for mentors who have had success in these areas. Be intentional in terms of who you choose and how you serve them. And within the five areas for development, seek those who can help reinforce your values. Remember, who you learn from matters.

THE EARN PHASE

Let's now talk about the Earn phase. Success has a compounding effect. What you do early on benefits and multiplies for you later. Take agriculture, for example. As I have stated before, there are four processes: tilling the soil, planting the seed, watering or nurturing the growing plants, and harvesting the crop. You don't get a harvest without tilling soil, getting the soil ready, planting the seed, and nurturing it. It's a process. Each part builds on the success of the one that came before, almost like momentum.

When each process is completed correctly, there is a tremendous harvest. When you're in your Learn phase, make sure there are good soil and good seeds. If you do these things, the Earn phase can bring a plentiful harvest. It can be fun for you, because you get to see the fruit of your sacrifices and labor.

How do you get the greatest return in your earning years? Most people approach earnings only or mostly as what they can personally produce. But the greatest way to earn financially is by multiplying leaders.

Here's an example using a simple number as your current earnings. If you make more, multiply it, and if you make less, feel free to divide the number. Let's assume you're making $100,000 from the work you do. To continue to earn that amount, you need to show up every day and do that work. But if you multiply and develop leaders, and every one of them makes $100,000, that means you're probably earning a lot more money. By developing more leaders, you have a greater impact, leading to greater opportunities. Most people don't multiply leaders.

Let's break down how this works, once again using the five simple steps detailed in chapter 7.

- **Step 1:** I do the work. This is where most people have been in their careers, especially during the learning years.
- **Step 2:** I do it, and now someone is next to me.
- **Step 3:** They do it, and I'm next to them. I'm able to coach and mentor them. Step 3 is the hardest

and most expensive one. It requires time invested in others—time that could otherwise have been spent "producing," as in step 1. Having a long-term view is critical here.

- **Step 4:** Not only am I doing it, but they can do it and we both produce results. So, now we have two people who can produce results. Step 3 paid off twofold. This is the multiplying effect, correct? Wrong. This is addition.
- **Step 5:** Now I take the person I had next to me and put a new person next to them to go through the same five-step process. This is multiplication!

Most people don't do steps 4 and 5 well, so they only get the result of what they produce. Great leaders, however, perform addition and multiplication. They take one person and multiply that by ten people, twenty people, forty people, and more. The multiplying effect is the greatest way to increase your earnings years. It's not, "What can I produce?" but rather, "How can I develop more leaders who can reproduce?"

Let's talk more about developing leaders and the five steps outlined. As you move through steps 3, 4, and 5, it's important that you identify the right people to take that journey with you during the earning years.

John Maxwell's book *The Leader's Greatest Return* teaches a process for developing people that starts with identifying leaders. You do this by observing their behavior and interactions with others. Seek out those who demonstrate an ability to influence and inspire others toward common goals.

Next, invite them to the leadership table. Understand and connect with the leaders before you lead them. Motivate, encourage, train, and equip leaders to do their best. Doing this effectively will also attract more leaders, as people are drawn to those who want to help them grow. Finally, empower leaders and release them to fulfill their potential. Pair them up to develop and multiply other leaders. You can create a self-perpetuating cycle of growth and success that compounds for you if you follow through on all five steps. Be a compound leader.

THE RETURN PHASE

The final phase is Return, age sixty-one and above for me. If you recall our agricultural scenario, when you plant and water a seed, you can turn it into a bountiful harvest. Did you know that most people eat the seed? That's right—there is no Return after Earn. If you want to have a future harvest, keep planting seeds. Helping those coming up behind us will create a legacy of significance that will endure long after we're gone. This is the true difference

Success is about me, but significance is about others.

between success and significance. Success is about me, but significance is about others. Success is at the individual level, which is only part of the picture. However, significance is a sense of purpose and impact beyond you.

Return is a great time to revisit our five areas or capitals for development (FISHS): financial, intellectual, social, human, and spiritual. For most people, there is little to no financial capital in the early years—particularly during the Learn phase. But as we progress to each phase, financial assets typically grow. As a result, we become more influential. Are you seeing this come full circle? A person's gift opens doors to opportunities and puts them in the presence of influential people. In Return, you're now in a unique position to help others fulfill their giftedness.

One of the things Danielle and I put our time, effort, and resources (all five capitals) behind is our nonprofit called I AM Empowering. In partnership with The Maxwell Leadership Foundation, it aims to empower youth, equip future leaders, and transform communities. We do this by nurturing the leadership and entrepreneurial giftedness of teenagers (ages thirteen to eighteen) through partnerships with business and community leaders, celebrities, educators, and elected officials. In the Return years, you're in a unique position to do the same. Put your resources behind causes that will make a lasting difference.

Invest your *i*ntellectual capital in others as well. Consider the path most people take—a life of accumulated wisdom builds up to . . . retirement. You come to the pinnacle in your collective capital and choose to retire instead of return. All exponential growth of influence comes to a screeching halt. I understand why people do this. But what if you instead transitioned from Earn to Return, from doing work to mentoring?

I want to challenge you not to use the word *retire* but instead use *return*. We covered the value of mentorship at length throughout this text from the standpoint of receiving. It's now our responsibility to perpetuate the cycle of growth and give. Return what you have to invest in others.

We won't cover every other letter of FISHS at length, but as you can imagine, Return marks the peak of your capital across each. Let's take *s*ocial capital. Your network will likely be far-reaching. Bring mentees around and introduce them to people in your network. Open new doors for them to walk through and develop. You likely won't arrive at Return having gotten as far as you have without the help and support of others. Very few people are self-made. Be a person who helps others.

As for *h*uman capital, mentor and lead people in your strengths—don't mentor them in your weaknesses. This will enable them to go further than you did. Last, teach people how you created, designed, and built your life around values and traditions. This is *s*piritual capital you get to share with people who are in their Learn and Earn phases of life.

Return is a great time of reflection, which brings us to the full cycle of life and our three phases. Remember our earlier analogy: life can be a reservoir or a river for you. A reservoir is a body of water that has no life in it because it doesn't move. But a river is a body of flowing water. Because it flows, it carries life. Return is about continuing to flow freely and bring a new life of opportunities to others.

BRINGING IT ALL TOGETHER

Ideally, Learn, Earn, and Return is a sequential path that occurs in three phases of your life. However, it does not always work out that way. You may be embracing this concept for the first time but are tied up with what we call *life* and its many commitments—raising a family, paying a mortgage, and so on. Yet this process is highly effective regardless of where you currently are in your life. It may mean your experience ends up feeling more like three cycles at once. That's okay.

Learn tends to be a constant, especially if you commit to be a lifelong learner.

Earn can be lots of fun—the culmination of your hard-earned efforts.

Return is the most gratifying. You get to teach, mentor, and develop people. Return requires you to embrace these calls to action. Personally, writing this book is part of how I return.

Now it's your turn to take it forward. Let's develop more leaders, grow our influence, and expand the potential of ourselves and others. Start with Learn, transition to Earn, and move from success to significance with Return.

Fulfill Your Potential and Die Empty

There is a story from Myles Munroe's powerful book *Maximizing Your Potential* that illustrates the concept of living up to our maximum potential. It serves as a profound example of utilizing our capabilities.

MAXIMIZATION

As we dive into the message of our final chapter, I am reminded of the transformative impact this concept has had on my own life. There is a story from Myles Munroe's powerful book *Maximizing Your Potential* that illustrates the concept of living up to our maximum potential. It serves as a profound example of utilizing our capabilities.

Myles was invited to speak at a series of seminars in Germany over a three-month span. During that time, he was hosted by an incredible family, which allowed him to soak in the rich heritage of Deutschland. Among his experiences there was an encounter with Germany's famous autobahn, the open expressway with no speed limits that cuts across Germany and other neighboring countries.

Imagine the adrenaline surging through Myles's body as he wrestled with the responsibility of limitless power. It was his combined experience of speed limits, fear, and his knowledge of traffic laws versus this newfound freedom.

As he pressed the pedal, the speedometer hit 80 mph. Sure, he'd been driving for over twenty-five years, even reaching 90 mph occasionally. But there, he had an open invitation to push the limits. As other cars zoomed by, his speedometer passed 80 mph. Myles said that his host laughed and said, "What are you afraid of? We're still standing still."

Not one to back down, Myles pushed it further, reaching 115 mph. Pride surged in him as he raced through the mountains and the Black Forest. He said he felt like "the king of the road." As he passed car after car, his confidence grew. He found himself saying, "Why don't they pull over and let a real driver through?"

He had reached the pinnacle of driving. There was no one better. Then, out of nowhere, a Mercedes-Benz flew past him going at least 150 mph. His measly 115 mph suddenly felt slow, almost like he wasn't moving at all.

His host then delivered a reality check: "So you see, you're not traveling as fast as you can, but only as fast as you will."[52]

And there it is, a lesson from the autobahn for our lives: we're not traveling as fast as we can, but only as fast as we will.

Think about this for a moment. Myles Munroe was on the autobahn, driving faster than he'd ever gone before. He was filled with a feeling of power as his vehicle reached 115 mph, until another car flew by at 150 mph. This story is not about speeding; it's about the self-imposed limits that hinder our ability to maximize potential.

Consider the car Myles Munroe was driving. It was built to go 180 mph, yet Monroe wasn't comfortable going beyond 115 mph. The only thing that limited Myles Munroe was Myles Munroe. In the same way, we all are built with great power and potential. Each of us has a specific horsepower engine meant to be maximized. However, we typically won't maximize it because of our own self-limiting belief system.

We all have potential, but most people will never accomplish all that is possible for their lives because of the limits they put on themselves. Instead, the dreams, talents, wisdom, and visions of many remain dormant—unfulfilled, untapped, unshared, and unrealized. Rather than being brought forth into the world, potential is ultimately carried to the grave. As I shared earlier, this is precisely why Myles Munroe said the cemetery is the wealthiest place in the world.

Munroe's metaphor underscores what is possible for our lives. It's possible for us to rob the grave and die empty, fulfilling our potential. But it starts with you.

Munroe also said about potential, "The greatest threat to being all you could be is the satisfaction with who you are." Why stop short of realizing more possibilities for our lives? Don't be satisfied with traveling at 115 mph when you can go 180 mph. We must maximize to actualize our potential. Furthermore, Munroe argued, "One of the greatest tragedies in life is to watch potential die untapped. A greater tragedy is to watch potential live unreleased. How sad to know that the majority of the people on this planet will never discover who they really are, while others will settle for only a portion of their true self."[53]

> "The greatest threat to being all you could be is the satisfaction with who you are."
>
> —Myles Munroe

It is disheartening to see people consciously minimize their own potential, all while aiming for a dream of retirement. But as Munroe also pointed out, "Retirement is never a concept in the minds of world changers."[54] When we strive to maximize, we adopt a mindset that goes beyond the limitations of traditional thinking. This includes retirement, an idea that becomes irrelevant when we are committed to utilizing our full potential for the betterment of the world. A world changer brings nothing to the cemetery because there's no other way. Self-imposed limits, such as retirement, conflict with maximization.

Fulfilling our potential and dying empty ultimately brings change to the world. It means we pushed up against our boundaries. On the other hand, mediocrity lives well within the boundaries. It is the territory of life safely bounded on the north by compromise, on the south by indecision, on the west by lack of vision, and on the east by past thinking. When we compromise, we settle for less than our potential. Indecision keeps us in a state of stagnation. A lack of vision bounds us to drift aimlessly. And past thinking limits the perspective for what's possible in our lives.

Most of us live in mediocre territory. Are you living within those boundaries, or do you push up against them?

If *mediocre* means average—with half of the population above average and the other half below average—perhaps you're doing better than most. This means you're living outside mediocre territory, right? Wrong. One of the greatest deceptions that limits our lives is relative comparison. We may compare ourselves to others and think, *I'm better off than they are*, but true success is not measured by how much we have accomplished compared to what others have done. Rather, true success is a measure of what we've done compared to what was possible for us—what our potential allowed for. So, while we may outperform the average, we're still holding back on our gifts and talents.

AWAKEN TO YOUR POTENTIAL

Most the world has settled on mediocrity. However, I believe God expects more for your life. To avoid mediocrity, let us first *awaken* to the insidious traps that place limits on our lives. Myles Munroe referred to them as the thirteen enemies of potential.[55] I'll list them below but frame them in my own experience and observations.

Enemy #1: Opinions of Others

In the early part of my career, I allowed the opinions of others to define who I would be. I recall a mentor's words: "It's not possible to achieve what you want to do." Though I didn't entirely believe him, I also didn't fulfill what I knew I was capable of at the time. His opinion seeded some doubt. Thankfully, I realized opinions such as "you can't" or "you won't" rob us of our potential. Just because others can't see it doesn't mean our potential isn't real.

We must avoid giving undue weight to the opinions of others, for that elevates their design above God's design for our lives. Jeremiah 29:11 assures us of God's plans for our lives. I call this out not necessarily to push my faith but rather to make a statement: Consider the mistake of valuing the opinion of others over that of God's. Instead of maximization, we will find ourselves living unfulfilled lives. Whatever your faith may be, understand we are all capable of so much

Giving undue weight to the opinions of others mistakenly elevates their design above God's.

more—there is a higher calling for us. Don't let the cemetery win simply because of someone else's opinion for your life.

Enemy #2: Fear

Fear can take hold of our lives, robbing us of our potential. Consider some of the most common fears, ranging from losing your money to catching a disease. Statistically speaking, most of the things we fear never even happen. Consider the following: Researchers determined that 85 percent of what people worried about never happened. For those 15 percent whose worries came to fruition, 79 percent discovered they could deal with the difficulty better than they'd anticipated, some even learning a lesson during the process. When considered together, 97 percent of the things worried about either never happen, or if they do happen, people handle them well.[56] Not only will most of our worries never happen, but also 100 percent of what we worry about cannot be changed by worrying. Let's now put fear into perspective with the following acronym:

False Evidence Appearing Real

If you're overcome with fear, I encourage you to replace it with love, as seen in the following acronym:

Leave Others Valuable Experiences

Where fear is an enemy of potential, love releases it. Choose to leave others valuable experiences. It changed my life, and it will change yours. To leave room for others to have valuable experiences is to embrace an abundance mindset that says, "There's enough to go around." Moreover, love encourages.

> *If you're overcome with fear, replace it with love.*

Enemy #3: Discouragement

Discouragement kills human potential. When we surrender to it, common phrases tend to be, "I'm not moving forward," "I'm scaling back," or "I don't have what it takes." What these and many other phrases borne out of discouragement really mean is, "I'm going to stop going after my dreams."

You rarely hear children say that, do you?

Children never stop dreaming because they have yet to encounter the enemy of discouragement in such a powerful way. If we can rise above discouragement and perceive it as a stepping stone toward realizing our potential, we, too, can dream more freely. Doing so puts us in position to realize amazing results in life. Otherwise, discouragement will rob us of our dreams and bury untapped potential in the grave.

Enemy #4: Procrastination

Procrastination says we need to see every step of the journey, including all the events that need to fall into place. Action is delayed in favor of waiting for perfect conditions or absolute certainty. Those who fall prey to this enemy are robbed of reaching their potential because of the guise that any of this is true. We don't need to see the entire picture. Instead of delaying, we simply need to start walking or taking action. We gain greater clarity with each step, allowing us to see farther.

Procrastination is sneaky. We don't immediately recognize its harmful effects. But before we know it, the days, weeks, and months of putting something off add up to years. Procrastination may leave us years behind on fulfilling our potential, wondering where the time went.

When forms of procrastination surface in our minds, simply step forward. Start walking, and the picture will become more clear.

Enemy #5: Past Failures

In earlier chapters, I shared some of my past failures, which included declaring bankruptcy at the age of twenty-one. I've experienced a variety of other failures as well. In fact, I'm quite comfortable saying I've failed miserably over my lifetime. For years, I beat myself up for the mistakes of the past, buying into the lie that they defined my future. It eventually dawned on me that past failures don't have to stand as an enemy of potential. The realization that they didn't define my future set me free, and it can do the same for you.

Don't allow past failures to derail you from where you're meant to go in life. Convert past failures from enemies to allies by getting a return, or a lesson, from them. Improve and reenter. When we do this, we give ourselves permission to have a future that is brighter than our past.

Enemy #6: Distractions

Distractions are silent potential killers, robbing us of time, focus, and progress toward goals. Here are some examples:

- Social media: scrolling through newsfeeds and getting caught up with likes and comments
- Entertainment: spending hours binge-watching TV shows or playing video games

- Unproductive discussions: having meetings without clear outcomes or gossiping, especially when negative
- Multitasking: attempting to juggle many things, especially those that don't necessarily bring us closer to our purpose and vision

Distractions fragment our attention and pull us away from our potential. In some cases, they even falsely make us think we are busy or working hard. To fulfill our potential, we must minimize the distractions. Ask, "Does this bring me closer to fulfilling my potential?" If the answer is no, minimize or avoid it.

Enemy #7: Tradition

Tradition can be an enemy of potential when it is used to limit what we believe is possible. It can show up as dogma, such as, "We only do it this way," or, "It's always been done that way," leaving no room for other possibilities. This is another lie that, if bought into, threatens our potential. Consider all that exists in modern times today. If civilization always bought into "it's always been done this way," we would still be riding on horses and in carriages instead of in cars. Traditional thinking in the form of dogma robs us of our potential.

Enemy #8: Wrong Environment

In the wrong environment, we are surrounded by people who don't edify, grow, and stretch us to become the best versions of ourselves. I liken it to crabs in a bucket. Known as "crab mentality," when one attempts to climb out, the other crabs pull it back down. This is the wrong environment—one where others may hold you back and in some cases discourage or undermine your success. Instead of maximizing, we shrink back from our potential. This situation not only robs us but also future generations of what's inside us—the contributions we were designed to make in this world.

It serves us well to avoid the crab mentality. As we are the average of the people we spend the most time with, be mindful of who you surround yourself with. Those same people will shape your environment and define your future. If you want to be an eagle, fly with eagles. If you want to be a duck, then fly with ducks. But remember, ducks and eagles don't hang out together.

Enemy #9: Comparison

As I said earlier, comparison robs us of our potential. Don't compare yourself to others. Reach *your own* full potential. Take, for example, comparing a one-hundred-gallon gas tank to a ten-gallon one. If we have one hundred gallons of capacity, using anything over ten gallons creates a false reality of success. However, anything short of using all one hundred gallons robs us of our full potential.

Don't stop at ten gallons in life. If you have one hundred gallons, use it. Similarly, don't compare yourself to a one-thousand-gallon gas tank. This may engender feelings of frustration and inadequacy. We are far better off avoiding that.

Whatever our potential may be, we cannot compare it to others. Whether it's larger or smaller, the comparison itself will rob us. Instead, we must focus on and maximize what we have.

Enemy #10: Disobedience

Success follows obedience, particularly to God's laws. Whether you acknowledge them or not, those laws are relevant to your life. Take gravity, for instance. If you're standing atop a fifty-story building, defying gravity leads to an immediate encounter with its consequences. Belief or disbelief in God doesn't alter this truth.

Alternatively, obedience to those laws creates blessings. For example, Genesis 1:27 states we are created "in the image of God." God, therefore, places a "10" on our foreheads. "So in everything, do to others what you would have them do to you," according to Matthew 7:12. This Golden Rule calls for us to value every person, regardless of status, abilities, or what they can offer us. Most people are disobedient to this law.

But with obedience, the law states, "Ask and it will be given to you."[57] By treating others well, we fulfill God's commandments and invite favor and blessings into our

> *Obedience is not always about convenience; it requires diligence and maximizes brilliance.*

lives. For "a generous person will prosper; whoever refreshes others will be refreshed."[58] Disobedience, on the other hand, robs us of favor and blessings meant for our lives.

Obedience is not always about convenience; it requires diligence and maximizes brilliance.

Enemy #11: Opposition

Opposition is a close relative of distraction. When we declare to do something great, there's a phenomenon I've seen occur firsthand—the naysayers come out. All of a sudden, everyone wants to put a resistance up against you. If we believe and allow opposition to get in the way of what we want to achieve, opposition is going to rob us of our potential. Whatever we are meant to bring to the world instead gets carried to the grave.

The opposition is always there, trying to stand in the way. There are going to be some people who will be against what we want to accomplish. But when we keep moving forward, the opposition eventually steps aside and out of the way.

Opposition doesn't deserve our attention because whatever we focus on expands. If we place our attention on the opposition, it expands. But if we instead put attention on our purpose and vision, guess what happens? That expands. We are more likely to rob the grave and bless the world with our potential fulfilled. Don't waste focus on the opposition. The opposition puts up a fight, but attention to goals brings them to flight.

Enemy #12: Societal Pressures

Society will put pressure on us, especially in the field of academia. It says that we have to be good at everything. This is a lie. Consider if we try to chase six rabbits. We'll catch none of them. But if we pick one and chase it, we'll catch that rabbit. In the same way, society tells us to chase everything at once, and we end up with nothing.

The most successful people in the world are not good at everything. They're good at a few things and they dominate those areas. We, too, can pick one or two strengths and dominate them. Put weaknesses to the side, because no one pays for them. We never hear, "I want a mediocre financial advisor," or "I'm looking for an average doctor." Focus on your unique giftedness, refine it, and bring it to the world.

Enemy #13: Success

This last enemy is probably the most important one. The thirteenth enemy of our potential is success. When most people are trying to grow, they apply discipline, sacrificing today for a better tomorrow. But once they get what they want, that sacrifice goes away.

As we started seeing success, Danielle and I had to make a conscious decision to be intentional and disciplined

> *Put success in its place: enjoy it for twenty-four hours, and then move forward.*

to achieve more. We saw examples of the opposite: those who tasted success and became complacent—partying, eating, drinking, and becoming lackadaisical in their lifestyle. Suddenly, their potential for more was robbed. But if our goal is to fulfill our potential and eventually die empty, it does not serve us well to fixate on the wins along the way.

Don't allow successes to equate to identity. Put success in its place: enjoy it for twenty-four hours, and then move forward. If we follow this advice, success will not rob us of our potential.

BE EMPOWERED TO REACH YOUR POTENTIAL

Potential is like a seed: if you eat a fruit and the seed that's inside it, there's no more potential. That's because the potential resided in the seed. When you eat it, there's nothing left to sow. Most people eat the seed in their life and don't invest or reinvest to reach their full potential.

For us to reach our potential, rob the grave, and die empty, we must never eat all the seeds. It's okay to enjoy some of the fruits of our labor, but it's imperative that we keep reinvesting, growing, developing, and challenging what's possible for our lives. To *empower* and reach our potential, we must continue to grow into it.

Consider the farmer's process once more:

Preparing the Soil: Just as a farmer prepares the soil to create optimal conditions for growth, preparing the soil of our potential involves creating an atmosphere for its realization. Develop a positive mindset, our greatest ally that will empower us against any of the thirteen enemies of potential. To refuse to buy into naysayers' opinions, overcome fear, resist discouragement, and avoid procrastination is to create the right environment for growth.

Sowing the Seed: Sowing the seed represents taking deliberate action toward our goals. This is us stepping out in faith to plant the seed of potential. Just as a farmer plants seeds with purpose and intention, we, too, must take steps toward realizing our potential. This involves being intentionally good—putting actions behind good intentions.

Watering the Harvest: Watering the seed symbolizes consistent effort, dedication, and perseverance with the expectation of a bountiful harvest. Just as each drop of water is expected to nurture the seed's growth, every step we take should be with the expectation to fulfill our potential.

Most people don't reach their potential because they don't expect to succeed. But consider this: a farmer doesn't water the seed and hope for a harvest. If a tomato seed is planted, the farmer expects a tomato to harvest. Planting comes with a clear expectation. Similarly, once we start walking, expect the picture to become clear. Expect success; don't wish for it. Develop, grow, and challenge yourself, knowing that you *will* rob the grave and die empty.

Harvesting the Crop: Harvesting the crop signifies reaping some of the rewards of our efforts and seeing the manifestation of our potential. Just as a farmer gathers the fruits of their labor, we, too, can celebrate our successes. Just remember, don't eat all the seeds.

People often use the saying "God willing" to express uncertainty and the need to remain humble in acknowledgment of divine oversight. Well, I'd add that "God is willing. Are you?"

I'm sometimes asked how I can be so confident in my expectations. As a person of faith, it's because I know what my heavenly Father has shared with me. God is faithful to complete it. Just as our farmer has certainty in the process, so must you. If we plant a seed in the ground, water it, and provide it with sunlight, it will bear fruit that we'll harvest. The same applies to reaching our potential and dying empty. Embrace the process of fulfilling your potential. By developing, growing, and continuously taking forward action, the harvest will happen in our lives.

BE EQUIPPED TO FULFILL YOUR POTENTIAL

Just as a farmer uses tools to toil the ground and plants seeds in anticipation of a harvest, we can use tools to help us reach our potential. We can be *equipped* with tools that identify giftedness, raise the lid on leadership, and enable us to create multiplication through our engagement with others. There's likely no shortage of advice available on how best to do this. That said, I encourage you to utilize the following six tools to reach your potential.

Tool #1–Leadership Assessment for Mission, Competency, and Style

As I've discussed throughout this book, operating from an area of strength, our giftedness, enables the greatest release of potential. This is because no matter how much we improve in an area of weakness, we'll never go as far as we can in our giftedness. For these reasons, my companies leverage an online leadership assessment to identify an individual's giftedness across the following three parameters:

Mission = What You're Passionate About (Your What)
Competency = What You're Good At (Your Why)
Style = How You and Others Perceive You (Your How)

After so many years of trial and error, I can confidently say the online assessment I use provides the highest probability of someone reaching their potential. Simply put, when we know our giftedness, we're better equipped to spend our time and energy refining it. Doing so yields the greatest return.

Tool #2–Emotional Intelligence Assessment

High emotional intelligence is associated with a deep understanding of and appreciation for the complexities of human interactions. It is no wonder 90 percent of top performers have high emotional intelligence. According to Multi-Health Systems' Emotional Quotient Inventory 2.0 (EQ-i 2.0), one of the most widely used emotional intelligence tests, there are five key areas worth paying attention to: self-perception, self-expression, interpersonal skills, decision-making, and stress management.[59] If we neglect these areas, they could become roadblocks that limit our potential.

We can cultivate high emotional intelligence through emotional intelligence assessments. I encourage you to find one that assesses your strengths across these areas. Awareness of each area affords us the opportunity to address and convert them from would-be roadblocks to allies.

Tool #3—The 21 Irrefutable Laws of Leadership Course

Offered through our leadership coaching company, Lions Pride Leadership (LPL), this online course delivers the lessons of John Maxwell's book *The 21 Irrefutable Laws of Leadership* in digital form. It serves as a valuable guide to the major principles of leadership, including how to connect with and influence people, empower others, and build an all-star leadership team.

The course is taught by John Maxwell, me, and others. Speaking from personal experience, the lessons from each of the twenty-one laws will equip you to raise your leadership lid and unlock your full potential.

Tool #4–8 Steps to Developing People Course

If we take care to master the eight steps to developing people, we will release our own potential as well as the potential of those we lead. That's because to fulfill our own potential is to release it in others. Let's review each of the below, which are covered in an online course through LPL as well.

1. *You are here*: Acknowledging where we are in our leadership journey. For example, we can't take people where we haven't gone, and we can't lead them if we don't know where we are.

2. *Identify*: Identifying great people. Know what greatness looks like and to able to tell when a great person walks by.

3. *Awareness*: Becoming aware of what our liabilities are and what's holding us back from our potential. These could be the thoughts, beliefs, or behaviors that shape our results. The same awareness applies to helping others.

4. *Giftedness*: Identifying our giftedness, as it opens up doors and puts us in front of influential people. Operating in our area of strength releases the greatest potential.

5. *Styles*: When the heart is right, the hand, the head, and the habits are right. We want to make sure that we get the heart right—everything else flows from there.

6. *Character*: There are dividers, subtracters, adders, and multipliers. Character is about how we intentionally become a multiplier. A multiplier exponentially increases their influence, impact, opportunities, revenue, profit, and much more.

7. *Motivation*: Understanding what drives one person versus another.

8. *Journey*: Recognizing and reminding ourselves that fulfillment of potential is a lifelong journey. Success does not happen overnight.

Tool #5—Business Model Alignment (BMA)

Covered in chapter 3 and revisited here, the Business Model Alignment (BMA) is a tool I teach to business leaders across the globe. It helps them develop an effective business strategy across the following six principles:

1. *Purpose*: Why our business exists

2. *Vision*: Where we are going

3. *Values*: Ideals that are nonnegotiable and not to be compromised

4. *Giftedness*: The areas of strength for our key leaders

5. *Strategy*: The intentional plan to accomplish the purpose and vision

6. *Metrics*: What we use to keep our people accountable

Regardless of its nature, creating total alignment for our line of work or business enhances our leadership. And as we now well know, leadership ability and potential go hand in hand.

Tool #6—Master Operating System (MOS)

The last tool, also taught to business leaders through the Lions Pride Leadership platform, is the Master Operating System (MOS). This includes eight areas every business needs to focus on as part of an overall strategy. The right level of focus on each ensures success for an organization because it provides scalability. An effective MOS allows people the freedom to take on responsibility, be creative, and make decisions. People can manage themselves and maximize within clearly defined boundaries, while leadership can continuously refine the system. In turn, great organizational potential is released.

1. *Vision*: Setting a clear vision that each team member can clearly articulate, from core values that attract talent to a strategy that aligns people's efforts today and in the future. A true vision will always build others up rather than pull them down.

2. *Language*: Placing emphasis on what we say and how we say it within an organization. When there's commonality and consistency in the language an organization uses, it creates trust and alignment. The language we share ultimately shapes our future. Therefore, language should reflect the intent of an organization's purpose, vision, values, and strategy.

3. *Systems*: Creating procedures, processes, methods, or courses of action designed to achieve a specific result. These are a set of principles for how something is done. When done well, systems allow for scalability, consistency, improved efficiency, and increased overall fulfillment.

4. *Metrics*: Collecting and organizing data is a vital component of every business. That said, we must take great care to measure what counts. The right metrics, which can be referenced continuously, allow for quality decision-making and increase the probability of winning over the long run.

5. *People*: Establishing a teamwork culture, team building activities, and a plan for developing the greatest asset to a business—it's people.

6. *Issues*: Putting in place practices to mitigate as well as intentionally address issues (people and systems) as they arise (and they will). An efficient organization addresses issues immediately, but it does so in a way that fosters growth and goodwill among its people.

7. *Customers*: Understanding and refining the customer experience through their interaction with the business at hand. This includes how you engage and exchange with customers today and tomorrow (for example, exchange in abundance), who your existing customers are (current characteristics), which customers you want to attract in the future (ideal characteristics), and building a plan to reach new customers (to achieve greater results) in the future.

8. *Glue*: Intentionally good actions that move an organization in the direction of its purpose, vision, values, and strategy. It drives transparency

and accountability from top to bottom, through one-on-ones, team meetings, networking events, and town halls (to name a few). Like actual glue, it helps maintain strong connections and fosters ownership among individuals and teams alike. Glue keeps all the areas of the MOS together.

A meaningful MOS should reflect how a business runs each and every day. Everything should fall into place when we focus on building an effective one. We become better leaders, our people add more value, and our organizations become more valuable.

FULLY AWAKENED, EMPOWERED, AND EQUIPPED

When the farmer uses tools to toil the ground, he knows the harvest is coming. Likewise, any combination of our six tools will ensure a harvest of abundance in your life. You may decide to use some or all of them. If you only select a few, I encourage you to leverage our leadership and emotional intelligence assessments. Understanding who we are and how we operate has the power to change everything. But regardless of your choice, one thing is certain: each tool releases potential.

Having experienced a great awakening, we are now empowered to move boldly toward reaching our highest level of achievement. The next step is fulfillment—you are also fully equipped to make the most of your talents, skills, and abilities with nothing held back. Remember, fulfillment leaves nothing in the tank. It's time to embrace your potential, avoid its thirteen enemies, reinvest the seed, and see your efforts bear fruit.

My friend, rob the grave and die empty!

MORE WAYS TO AWAKEN YOUR POTENTIAL

Imagine the impact on someone else's life when you share this book. Join us in awakening the potential in others. Here are some things you can do:

1. Leave a review of the book at your favorite online bookstore.

2. Share the book and your story on social media. Uses the hashtag #awakenyourpotential

3. Give someone a copy of this book and let them know how it has changed you.

4. Meet face-to-face or send a note to a friend and tell them how much you loved the book.

5. Be a multiplier! Teach someone the life-changing principles you've learned.

6. Help someone dive deeper into this message by sharing our leadership articles and videos.

For Leadership Videos   For Leadership Articles

Unlock more resources by using this additional QR code. Simply scan to delve deeper into the insights and references provided within these pages.

Let your journey to unlock your fullest potential continue!

ACKNOWLEDGMENTS

A special thank you to . . .

My mother, from whom I learned the power of love and vision, and my late father, from whom I learned the power of discipline and unwavering dedication. Thank you both for your love and sacrifices to make me the man I am today.

Waikiki Paulino, for challenging me to be a better man, husband, friend and follower of Jesus. The impact your commitment made on me in my early walk with God is almost impossible to put into words. It awakened my potential and for that reason, I am forever grateful to you.

Rob and Ann-Marie Lopez, who provide friendship, prayer, and support to ensure we collectively impact more lives together! Danielle and I are forever grateful to you both.

Matt Stern, my writing partner who helped take what was in my heart and mind and put it on paper to help this message reach more people. Forever grateful to you.

ABOUT THE AUTHOR

Chad L. Reyes is a purpose-driven entrepreneur, coach, speaker, author, and multiplier of leaders. Since 2003, he has worked with CEOs, entrepreneurs, business leaders, highly successful families, and the next generation of leaders to reach their full potential.

His journey from declaring chapter 7 bankruptcy at twenty-one years old to influencing highly successful leaders all started with a vision for how he and his wife, Danielle, would one day ignite positive change in the world. Dedicating their lives to that vision, they have pioneered three organizations focused on developing leaders:

> *Lions Pride Leadership*, a leadership and business coaching company that awakens, empowers, and equips leaders to reach their full potential.
>
> *I AM Empowering*, a not-for-profit organization that empowers and equips the next generation of

leaders, focusing on those between the ages of thirteen and eighteen.

Wealth & Legacy Group, a generational planning firm that helps highly successful families move from success to significance.

Chad's motto, inspired by Myles Munroe, is simple: *Rob the grave and give the world everything you have inside. Die empty.*

To learn more, visit ChadReyes.com.

ENDNOTES

Chapter 1

1. James Clear, *Atomic Habits: An Easy & Proven Way to Build Good Habits & Break Bad Ones* (New York: Avery, 2018), 69–71.
2. Gary Hamel and C. K. Prahalad, "Strategic Intent," *Harvard Business Review*, July–August 2005, https://hbr.org/2005/07/strategic-intent.
3. John C. Maxwell, *Intentional Living: Choosing a Life That Matters* (New York: Center Street, 2015), 47–48.
4. Adapted from Loren Eiseley, "The Star Thrower," in *The Unexpected Universe*, 1969.

Chapter 2

5. "Lois Hirschman: A Tale of a Girl Scout 80 Years Green," Girl Scouts of the USA, accessed October 26, 2023, https://www.girlscouts.org/en/our-stories/parents-and-volunteers/volunteers/lois-hirschman-girl-scout-80-years-green.html.
6. Officevibe Content Team, "Statistics on the Importance of Employee Feedback," öfficevibe, October 7, 2014, https://officevibe.com/blog/infographic-employee-feedback.

7. Naz Beheshti, "10 Timely Statistics About the Connection Between Employee Engagement And Wellness," *Forbes*, January 16, 2019, https://www.forbes.com/sites/nazbeheshti/2019/01/16/10-timely-statistics-about-the-connection-between-employee-engagement-and-wellness/.

8. Tony Schwartz and Christine Porath, "Why You Hate Work," *New York Times*, March 30, 2014, https://www.nytimes.com/2014/06/01/opinion/sunday/why-you-hate-work.html.

9. S. Mutha, C. Allen, and M. Welch, *Toward Culturally Competent Care: A Toolbox for Teaching Communication Strategies* (San Francisco, CA: Center for Health Professions, University of California, 2002).

10. Jack Zenger and Joseph Folkman, "The 3 Elements of Trust," *Harvard Business Review*, February 05, 2019, https://hbr.org/2019/02/the-3-elements-of-trust.

Chapter 3

11. "Publisher Description for Man's Search for Meaning / Viktor E. Frankl," Library of Congress Catalog, accessed October 26, 2023, https://catdir.loc.gov/catdir/enhancements/fy0628/2006287144-d.html.

12. Naina Dhingra et al., "Help Your Employees Find Purpose—Or Watch Them Leave," McKinsey & Company, April 5, 2021, https://www.mckinsey.com/capabilities/people-and-organizational-performance/our-insights/help-your-employees-find-purpose-or-watch-them-leave.

13. "About Us," Nordstrom, accessed October 26, 2023, https://press.nordstrom.com/about.

14. "About Us," Nordstrom.

15. John Maxwell, *The 21 Irrefutable Laws of Leadership: Follow Them and People Will Follow You*, rev. ed. (New York: HarperCollins Leadership, 2007), 209.

Chapter 4

16. Jim Harter, "Employee Engagement vs. Employee Satisfaction and Organizational Culture," Gallup, updated August 13, 2022, https://www.gallup.com/workplace /236366/right-culture-not-employee-satisfaction.aspx.
17. Stephen Covey, *The 7 Habits of Highly Effective People*, (New York: Simon & Schuster, 1989), 305.
18. "Who We Are: Corporate Purpose," Chick-fil-A, accessed October 26, 2023, https://www.chick-fil-a.com /about/who-we-are.
19. Gary Chapman and Paul White, *The 5 Languages of Appreciation in the Workplace: Empowering Organizations by Encouraging People* (New York: Northfield Publishing, 2011).
20. Acts 20:35.

Chapter 5

21. Nation's Restaurant News. "Chick-Fil-A Ranked No. 1 for Customer Satisfaction for the 9th Straight Year," June 27, 2023. https://www.nrn.com/consumer-trends/chick -fil-ranked-no-1-customer-satisfaction-9th-straight -year; information can also be found at https://theacsi .org/?s=chick+fil+a.
22. Meghan Overdeep, "The Average Chick-fil-A Restaurant Tops McDonald's, Starbucks, and Subway in Sales," *Southern Living*, April 4, 2019, https://www.southern living.com/news/chick-fil-a-sales-per-restaurant.

23. More about Chick-fil-A's giving philosophy can be found at https://www.chick-fil-a.com/about/giving-back.

24. Max Phillips, "Why Only 8% of People Achieve Their Goals, According to Research," Medium, September 14, 2020, https://medium.com/the-ascent/why-only-8-of-people-achieve-their-goals-according-to-research-998198f84cf.

25. This quote is found often on the internet; it is likely from one of his sermons.

26. Ray Williams, "Too Many Choices and Decision-Fatigue," Medium, November 28, 2021, https://raybwilliams.medium.com/we-face-too-many-choices-and-decision-fatigue-df2d41d0bd8e.

27. Williams, "Too Many Choices and Decision-Fatigue."

28. John Maxwell, *The 21 Irrefutable Laws of Leadership: Follow Them and People Will Follow You*, rev. ed. (New York: HarperCollins Leadership, 2007), 64–65.

29. Stephen Newland, "The Power of Accountability," AFCPE, 2018, https://www.afcpe.org/news-and-publications/the-standard/2018-3/the-power-of-accountability/.

30. Newland, "The Power of Accountability."

31. Myles Munroe, *Maximizing Your Potential: The Keys to Dying Empty* (Shippensburg, PA: Destiny Image Publishers, Inc., 2008), 146.

Chapter 6

32. Tasha Eurich, "What Self-Awareness Really Is (and How to Cultivate It," *Harvard Business Review*, January 4, 2018, https://hbr.org/2018/01/what-self-awareness-really-is-and-how-to-cultivate-it.

33. Genesis 1:27.

34. This framework was developed by Verna Cornelia Price in her book, *The Power of People: Four Kinds of People Who Can Change Your Life* (JCAMA Publishers, 2003).

35. Copyright 2011 by Multi-Health Systems Inc. Based on the original BarOn EQ-i authored by Reuven Bar-On, copyright 1997, https://storefront.mhs.com/collections /eq-i-2-0.

Chapter 7

36. Adapted from Edgar Dale's cone of experience model (1954), National Training Laboratories Institute (NTL) for Applied Behavioral Science, Learning Pyramid, accessed October 27, 2023, https://www.educationcorner .com/the-learning-pyramid.html.

37. I tried to find where I first heard this teaching, but I have heard it so much through the years, and it has become such a part of my life, that I know it by heart.

38. John C. Maxwell, *The Leader's Greatest Return: Attracting, Developing, and Multiplying Leaders* (New York: HarperCollins Leadership, 2020), 86.

39. Ken Blanchard and Phil Hodges, *Lead Like Jesus* (Nashville, TN: Thomas Nelson, 2005).

40. Rick Warren, *The Purpose Driven Life: What on Earth Am I Here For?* (New York: Zondervan, 2012), 21.

Chapter 8

41. The story of the creation of *Rocky* has been covered so many times in so many ways. I have put the facts together as best I remember. If you want to know more, Google it. Just be prepared to lose yourself down that rabbit hole.

42. Peg Moline, "We're Far More Afraid of Failure Than Ghosts: Here's How to Stare It Down," *Los Angeles Times*, October 31, 2015, https://www.latimes.com/health/la -he-scared-20151031-story.html.

43. "Findings from Our CEO Journey Study," Norwest Venture Partners, August 22, 2018, https://www.nvp.com /blog/insights-norwests-2018-ceo-journey-study/.

44. "Steve Jobs," AZ Quotes, https://www.azquotes.com /quote/147189.

45. "Bill Gates," Brainy Quote, https://www.brainyquote .com/authors/bill-gates-quotes.

46. Mark Cole. "Mark Cole: The Difference Between Average and Achieving - John Maxwell." John Maxwell, February 4, 2020. https://www.johnmaxwell.com /blog/mark-cole-the-difference-between-average-and -achieving/.

47. Mark 2:22.

48. "Zig Ziglar," AZ Quotes, https://www.azquotes.com /quote/325065.

Chapter 9

49. Christine Comaford, "76% of People Think Mentors Are Important, but Only 37% Have One," Forbes, July 3, 2019, https://www.forbes.com/sites/christinecomaford /2019/07/03/new-study-76-of-people-think-mentors-are -important-but-only-37-have-one/?sh=719d900a4329.

50. Matthew 7:7.

51. "Jim Rohn," Goodreads, https://www.goodreads.com /author/quotes/657773.Jim_Rohn.

Chapter 10

52. Myles Munroe, *Maximizing Your Potential: The Keys to Dying Empty* (Shippensburg, PA: Destiny Image Publishers, Inc., 2008), 28–29.

53. Munroe, *Maximize Your Potential*, Introduction, 28–29.

54. Munroe, *Maximize Your Potential*, 28–29.

55. Munroe, *Maximize Your Potential*, Chapter 3, pgs. 57–76.

56. Don Joseph Goewey, "85 Percent of What We Worry About Never Happens," HuffPost, August 25, 2015, https://www.huffpost.com/entry/85-of-what-we-worry-about_b_8028368.

57. Matthew 7:7.

58. Proverbs 11:25.

59. "EQ-i 2.0," Multi-Health Systems Inc., accessed October 28, 2023, https://storefront.mhs.com/collections/eq-i-2-0.